PREDESTINED

Born for Greatness

ANDREY SHAPOVAL

ISBN-13: 978-1-7908-2545-5

Preface

Dear friend,

Your choice to read this book is not an accident. Before the words
on this page began to come together, I prayed for you. I pray that
by reading this book, the Holy Spirit will renew your
understanding of all things and reveal to you your true identity.
You are a child of God. A victorious, faith-full, new person in
Christ through whom many people are impacted, influenced, and
ultimately, changed. My only desire is for Jesus Christ Himself to
edify you. He came into the world to give light to anyone who
believes and who continues to believe today. While reading the
words comprising this unique book, the Holy Spirit will begin to
change your way of thinking. It may be an unexpected change,
yet, at the same time, it will be the best kind of change to take
place. Stay with me, friend, and follow along closely. Your life
transformation is at hand. I pray the most personable individual,
The Holy Spirit, will forever change you by opening the eyes of
your heart and allowing you to see yourself through the light of
God. In the Lord Jesus Christ, you possess a rich and glorious
inheritance.

Right now, I want something new to take place inside your heart.
Allow time to stand still, if even for an instant, and let God take
you back to the moment when He conceived you. Before your
lungs filled with air as your cry announced your entrance to the
world, God already filled your life with His plans. Before any of
your days began, He already mapped out every single one of
them. Before He formed you within your mother's womb, He
created you in His mind! [26] I have come to know the orchestration
of God never plays its part in the visible realm until He brings it to
a finish in the spiritual realm. Your existence on earth is a direct
confirmation that God completed your destiny on earth. Your
human birth has taken place in the physical realm because God

has already finalized your fate in the spiritual realm. He longs for you to become a person after His heart, a person who accomplishes His will and the intentions He destined for your days in this generation. He called you for such a time as this. As is written about John the Baptist, God used this man to invite people to repent and believe in Jesus Christ. John carried out his role and you and I have our own to fulfill. We must use this time to seek and serve God, never forgetting we exist because of him. Every breath we take is from Him and only in Him do we live, move, and have our being.

From the moment I felt compelled to put my thoughts on paper, I prayed you would specifically become a person of faith through whom many people will be changed. As you walk through the days of your life, your destiny and calling will ignite the hearts of those around you and spread the Kingdom of God like wildfire. Trust me when I say, these pages are not mere information. This book is about a powerful revelation from the Holy Spirit, which radically changed my life. These chapters will walk you through my spiritual, God-given journey. As you read, my friend, remember that if God did this to my heart, He can do the same to yours. He can ignite it with fire, passion, and a hunger for something more. You are born for greatness. Your breath and body are God-given and hold a greater purpose than you even know. He wants to use you and me to continue writing His Acts on earth. The depths of my heart cry out to Him as I pray we would be a people of whom He is not ashamed to call Himself our God. I believe, through Him, we can complete this journey set for us, and as we bow down before Him on that glorious day, we will hear the words our hearts ache to hear, "Well done, good and faithful servant." If this is your prayer too, then join me on this journey with the Holy Spirit toward your destiny.

CONTENTS

ACKNOWLEDGMENTS

To say that I am grateful would be the least of what I truly feel toward those who joined me on this journey to publish my first book. Using this wonderful opportunity, I would like to thank all the people who made it possible.

Natasha, my beautiful wife stood by my side through it all, supporting my decision to leave the city to put thoughts into words. She never discouraged God-given dreams. Family is precious and highly cherished. Without lacking anything, confidently I write together we endured a busy season as the book came together.

What a joy it has been to work with Kristina Kovalevich, who self-willingly quit her day job, moving to Hawaii for several months to translate and transcribe audio content. As a ghostwriter, she remained faithful to this entrusted project. It is undeniable this book would not be published in a timely manner without her sacrifice.

Yuriy and Kristina Knysh have been nothing less than a blessing to my family and our team at Flame of Fire Ministry. Thank you for investing financially and being part of making this book happen. Your commitment has not gone unnoticed.

The main editorial work was done by Inna Chelak, who is gifted to creatively transform basic phrases into captivating sentences, that stay with the reader long after reading. Countless number of hours and weeks was sown into this project. Sincerely thankful for your collaboration and openness.

Final touches and valuable raw input were given by Jenny Soldatenkov. Her editorial eye helped elevate this project to the level we all envisioned it to be, bringing liveliness to every chapter. A thousand thanks for ensuring everything to flow smoothly.

Thank you, Aleksey Kaznacheyev, for creatively designing the book cover. In addition, thankful for Vlad Vykhopen and Liana Vedernikov for assisting in this area.

Without the rest of Flame of Fire team, it would be difficult to complete just about anything. Appreciative for this talented group of people.

Introduction

The atmosphere shifted. Closing my eyes, I inhaled deeply and exhaled slowly. The air, laced with heaviness, compressed my frame. In an instant, my body lifted up above the earth, transporting me to a different dimension. My eyes flew open as I floated above the ground. Focusing on my surroundings, I found myself inside an enormous building. The ceiling hovered above me with no walls holding up the structure. There was no end as the factory-like construction stretched all around me. Heavy machines occupied the never-ending space while workers labored at their stations. Much of the equipment stood empty, workforce scarce.

I continued to watch from above, the birds-eye view offering a unique perspective. A plethora of work to complete but a shortage of staff proved this a difficult feat to accomplish. In a frenzy, the available workers scurried between their current station and all the empty stations in their vicinity in an attempt to fulfill all the functions of each post. Ceaselessly they cried out, '*Help! We need help!*'

My heart clenched inside my chest at their desperate pleas. Severely understaffed, I understood they would never be able to finish the work. If there were only enough people to fill each station, quality work could be complete in time for distribution.

The conveyor belt hummed as it rolled out more and more work. My head spun with the realization of the immense need for laborers in such a massive factory with countless machines. The cries of the people pierced my heart. I pleaded with God on behalf of the workforce, *'Where is everyone? Why are there missing workers?'*

Slowly turning to my right, I peered inside a wide hallway. An obscenely overweight person, neither man nor woman, paced back and forth. It heard the frantic call of the workers but kept treading, ignoring the distressed cries for help. My thoughts raced, *'Who is this person?'* Right then, the Holy Spirit began to speak.

CHAPTER ONE

STEPS

May 2002, a breeze gently brushed my face as I sat on the steps of the apartment complex that spring evening. I would often sit on these steps and contemplate life, allowing my thoughts to wander freely. This was my usual escape. A place where I disconnected from reality and sank into my inner being. Little did I know this evening would be significantly different from any other I have ever experienced.

Diving deep into the vast ocean of my thoughts, I swam through endless streams as they all battled for my attention. The realization of just how average everyone lived their life pressed into my mind and left me unsettled. There had to be more to life. There had to be more to my story, what could it be? The uncertainty of what the future held pushed me on every side. In an unexpected instant, an inner battle broke out. My mind became a combat zone as two entirely different voices fought to the forefront.

Never had I imagined someone could dig so deep into their soul and yet here I was, barely holding on, as reality grew vague and I began to understand this was no longer a fight of my flesh. In a split second, my body shuddered and I was now certain this was a spiritual battle. Two sides were at war for my soul. My spirit cried out in utter desperation from the heaviness of all my anxieties. My so-called *life* was hanging by a string; tangled in situations I had no idea how to untie.

Everyone talks about a turning point and I can undeniably say this was my moment. I had stepped into my Garden of Gethsemane. As I sat on those stairs, I knew a fierce war waged for my future. I felt like Jacob, wrestling and fighting to secure his blessing. [21] It was the most surreal feeling. As the struggle continued, I understood I was not fighting one battle, but two. A battle with God, for my blessing, and another against the devil.

Two images slowly appeared in my mind's eye. One of my past. Mistakes. Regrets. The other full of questions and a hunger for answers to what lay ahead in my journey. *Who am I? Why am I here? Why was I born? What comes next? Is this really it?* At a mere twenty-two years of age, I felt as though I was completely void of any purpose to offer this world. I glanced down into the dry well of my existence, hoping to find at least a drop of hope, anything to shine a ray of light into my future. I came up dry, finding nothing. I had hit rock bottom and my feelings portrayed it. I felt no satisfaction or joy. Nothing but the pounding of my heart as everything within me desperately cried out to God. *What next Lord? How can I possibly go on like this?* The thoughts roared like a raging river, intensifying as it drew closer and closer. All of a sudden, a dreamlike stillness emanated. It was as if the river finally joined the ocean. The chaos abruptly stopped and I heard the faint voice of my mother, "Andrey, God brought you here for a purpose."

I had a purpose? A flood of hope rose within me at the sound of my mother's voice and childhood memories slowly emerged in my mind. My mother had once told me the miraculous story about the beginning of my life. She had been sleeping and in her dream, she remembered a silhouette of a man take shape behind her. In a very firm and audible voice, she heard him say, "On the 17th day of the month, the number of your family will change. You will give birth to a son and I want you to name him Andrey." Just like that, the dream was over and she woke, shaking. *Was this reality or just another dream*, she thought? She turned, waking my father, to relay the dream. His response gave her the assurance she needed, "If everything comes to pass the way it was said to you, and a son is born, then we will name him Andrey."

Living in the small village of Karotich, located within the Ukrainian City called Kharkiv, medical technology was limited with no opportunity to identify the gender of a fetus. On October 10th, my pregnant mother walked outside and was greeted by our neighbor, "Anna," she said, "I had a dream you gave birth to a boy." My mother strolled away with a smile playing across her face. A simple greeting yet with a profound confirmation of what she already knew. She would be on her way to deliver her baby the next day.

For the spoken word to take place, only a few short days remained before the birth and her arrival home with the newborn. She asked my father not go anywhere far, his nod signifying he would stay close for the delivery. A number of hours later, the contractions began. Grabbing the necessities, my parents rushed to the hospital as their anticipation grew. On October 11th, at 7:00 a.m., I took my first breath as my parents welcomed me into the world. They looked at each other and no doubt remained about my mother's dream. They named me Andrey and my days on this earth began.

The interesting part of this story is what followed shortly after. That Saturday, October 16th, my mother made

her way to view the discharge list, which displayed the
names of all the mothers who would be released the
following day. Not seeing her name, she walked back to her
room. Although the list did not show her name, she
remained confident; one way or another, she would go home
the next day, on the 17th, the spoken word fulfilled. It was
customary to keep the mother in the hospital for seven days
before discharging her to go home with the newborn. The
voice rang in her head, reminding her that the family would
change in number on the 17th day of the month. The same
evening, a janitor came to her, asking, "Anna, why are you
not packing your bags?" This was all the confirmation she
needed. The following day she walked through the doors of
our home, holding me in her arms. The timing was perfect;
God had done it again. God told Zechariah His spoken
words would come-to-pass in their appointed time. [1] Many
years later, and in a completely different situation, God's
words came to fruition in their appointed time, specifically
for my life.

This memory brought a surge of life into my weak bones
as I sat on those steps that evening. As pleasant as the
memory was, it faded into the night air and reality quickly
crept back in. The difficulty of my situations weighed me
down. I was not facing simple obstacles. I had lost
everything. The devil had used all my circumstances to put
me in a dead-end and push me away from the finish line. He
had filled my mind with negative thoughts and killed all of
my dreams along the way.

I felt hopeless again. The spark from before, once again,
blown out by regret. Both images reappeared as I sat there
trying to decide which one was meant for me. Lifting my
face to the heavens, my spirit cried out in the still of the
night. *Lord! Help me figure things out! Give me understanding*

and help me rise above these circumstances! I had no idea this particular evening would be a pivotal moment for the course of my life.

It had been a few short months since I gave my life to Jesus. I had finally admitted my helplessness and accepted Him as my Lord and Savior. Attempting to figure everything out on my own was proving difficult and my journal was full of problems I had yet to fix. As I sat there, the images of my old lifestyle raced across my mind. Hard as I tried, I could not find a way to make them disappear. The devil had returned to distract me. His arrows aimed for my mind as he tried to get me to look back at my old identity, which no longer held any power.

The two images stood before me and I knew I had to choose one. The image of my past or the image of my future. The decision was in my hands and this moment was crucial. I glanced at the staircase in front of me, realizing it held symbolic significance. God pointed out that step after step He could bring me up. He could pull me out from my circumstances and insecurities, which bound me. As I turned my focus from my past and to the future before me, I sighed heavily. *How did things get so out of hand?* I allowed my thoughts to travel back to my past and quickly realized my downhill tumble began long ago.

I felt utterly alone as I sat on those steps. I had grown used to the feeling of isolation.

Growing up, our neighbors constantly commented on our large family. They would say nothing good would ever become of us. With every memory, darts shot at me as I replayed their harsh words in my mind.

Our family immigrated to the states in 1995. Shortly after arriving to the new country, I rushed to build my music career. From an early age, God had given me the ability to play multiple instruments. I always knew writing music was a gift. Music consumed me. For as long as I can remember, I dreamed of becoming a professional musician, a famous composer. Somehow, I thought music would give my life purpose. I believed it could fill the gaping hole inside me. It did not take very long to see just how wrong I was. The more I sank into the music industry, the deeper my emptiness grew. Finding peace was difficult and nonexistent, and without God, I felt defeated.

As the years flew by, I grew distant from God. Sin took root in my life and spread into every corner of my being. The emptiness inside me was a constant ache. I began to realize nothing in this world truly brought any real satisfaction. My friends and I would gather and have a good time but I would leave feeling just as empty as before.

One summer night I made my way to a get-together, as I stood around with the guys, I heard the doorbell ring. My breath caught in my throat at the sight of her walking through the door. She was the most beautiful girl I had ever seen and I could not look away, mesmerized by the sway of her long blonde hair as she made her way into the crowd. At that moment, I promised myself I would do everything it took to get her attention. Being the gentleman I was, I walked over to introduce myself. Before long, we were lost in conversation. Dear, sweet Natasha. *This is the one!* I thought. *The woman of my dreams*. She could help me and finally fill the void.

The conversation threaded into countless others as our relationship developed and grew. Our dating years blissfully flew by in the blink of an eye until one night, I finally proposed to the love of my life. Our wedding date was set and everything seemed to be going forward as it should. Everything changed the day my best friend blew my cover.

A month before our big day, he met with Natasha and spilled the entire truth of who I really was. She quickly realized I was a hidden hypocrite.

I admit I knew how to play the part. The stage was familiar territory for me. I was the actor of my own platform and I had become a master at playing pretend. To be honest, I had no idea who I was at this point. I just carried on my show, as everything inside me lay dead. I now know that everything concealed will eventually come into light.

My worst nightmare began to play out as Natasha walked up to my doorstep, pulled off the engagement ring and flung it at my face.

"I will never build my life with a person who so easily lied to me," she declared. Turning around, she hurried back to her car. As I watched her drive away, my heart sank to the floor, completely shattered.

It was the lowest point of my life yet I still fought to hold control. The devil had succeeded in taking over everything and burning it to the ground. By then, I realized I had nothing left. In the preceding years, my life spiraled. The police had taken away my car. I had no way of paying for rent and quickly dug myself into a sinking hole of debt. My band was long gone and with it, any passion to write music. Before coming to Christ, I frequently drank in hopes of numbing my pain and fears. My last hope, of regaining any control, had been to marry Natasha. I had been sure she was the exact exit door I needed to run from all my problems. My final shot at anything meaningful and it was gone. In that season, God plucked out the last fiber I desperately held onto. My shaky foundation cracked and my life demolished. I was broken and unable to trust anyone. As Natasha's declaration replayed in my mind and agonizing pain poured from every corner of my heart, I ran out of the house. Drunk,

I drove around for hours, intoxicated by the alcohol rushing through my body as the pain grew in intolerable measure. With no idea how I would recover, I finally made my way home. Sleep overtook me, leaving me embarrassed and alone.

The following morning was Easter. Prying my eyes open, I knew I had to attend church. I was not going for any spiritual reasons. My only rationalization, for going, was to help my friend and his band lead worship that day. My reasoning centered on music, yet again. I had absolutely no idea God himself was drawing me in through the Holy Spirit. On April 1, 2002, God patiently waited as I made my way to the sanctuary.

Upon arrival, my friends informed me an evangelist, from Africa, would be to preaching the Easter sermon. After worship, I walked off the stage and quickly slid into the farthest pew I could find. I slumped into my seat, leaning my head against the wall. My thoughts carried me back to the previous night as I, again, replayed the mess my life had become. My attention moved to the evangelist. His sermon circled around Lazarus who had been dead in the tomb for four days. When Jesus came to resurrect him, the sisters of Lazarus warned Him not to open the grave because it had begun to stink. [2] I remember sitting there and suddenly becoming very alert when hearing this part of the story. The Holy Spirit began to show me I was Lazarus. Sin had clutched me and wrapped me in its bondage. Everything inside of me reeked. I was the dead man! The evangelist continued with his sermon, he spoke of Jesus, who silenced everyone and proceeded to call the dead Lazarus out of his grave. Something inside me trembled and it was as if the same stone rolled away from my heart! I began to see the slightest ray of hope.

"God," I whispered, "If you can, please resurrect me from the dead too." Suddenly, I heard a voice. In that instant, I understood the same Spirit who resurrected Lazarus, and the same Spirit who resurrected Jesus, had descended on me that Easter morning. God spoke directly to me and said, "Andrey, come out of this sinful life." That day was no longer just a celebration of the resurrection of Jesus; it was also the celebration of my own resurrection! I am a walking testimony that through the Holy Spirit, God holds the same resurrection power today to bring the dead back to life.

I wept as the evangelist called people to the front to receive Jesus. I found myself at the altar many times before. I asked for forgiveness but always returned to my old ways. Even still, something within assured me this time would be different. That was enough for me. I ran faster than I had ever run before and dropped to my knees in full surrender. I did not notice anyone around me, my focus drawn to the only One who mattered. With my arms raised to the heavens, my soul cried out to God in anguish and raw repentance.

During the altar call, the Holy Spirit tended to my wounds and I experienced the sweet love of the Father like never before. I do not remember how long I knelt at the altar, nor did I care. As I lifted my face, I looked up high and uttered my one request to the Lord, "God. For twenty-two years, I heard of you but I never knew you. From this day forward, I want to do everything in my power to truly know who you are!"

Despite being born in a Christian home, the faith of my family did not pass on through the generations. I had to make this decision personally. Both my father and mother loved God with their entire heart. To this day, my mother wholeheartedly serves the Lord. I truly believe every person must have a personal encounter with his or her creator.

My heart's cry led me on an adventurous journey with the Holy Spirit. Steadily, He began to lead me through life. He raised me to heights I could never attain on my own. Months had passed since that prayer, but my problems remained. Nothing seemed to be turning around.

Living in a house with my old roommates was a constant reminder of my past. Every day I had to make solid decisions to stand strong. I would beg God to keep me from returning to previous ways. This required me to drive away and spend time in prayer. Without silence, I could not seek God so I escaped to local parks to be alone. Time flew as I lost myself in the pages of the Bible. I knew this could not be a permanent solution; I could not keep running away to spend time with the Lord. I had to confront my roommates. They would have to choose between two options, remain and accept Jesus, or leave.

Walking back inside the house one afternoon, I shut the door to my room and began to pray. As my prayer grew louder and stronger, my roommates ran! They thought I went crazy and I did not care. The house was finally empty and I welcomed this new season of growth with God. I would often sit there and rewind the scenes of my life. My prayers to God continued. *Who am I, God, and why am I here?* The questions would come and go as my journey continued.

CHAPTER TWO

SUPERNATURAL

The steps, I sat on, represented my inner battle. Opening my eyes, the moonlight illuminated the sky above. A clear sign I had been sitting there awhile. Glancing at my watch, I saw it had become late. Immediately, every second began to matter. My attention shifted and my focus turned to how time progressed, reminding me that time always moves forward. Like the speed of a bicycle moving downhill, it moves onward quickly. Time is always accelerating and never looks back; every second attracts the future and only in this realm does it soar unbound.

My thoughts continued to invade every brain cell. They grew louder and louder as if someone had begun playing them through a megaphone, *time is going ahead, Andrey. Do not let your past hold you back from your future. The secret is in your mentality. Your thoughts will determine who you are.* I could not fully comprehend what I was hearing. A place in scripture sprang to mind and it rocked my understanding, "For I know the thoughts that I think toward you, says the Lord, thoughts of peace and not of evil, to give you a future and a hope." [3] The words anchored deep in my soul. The long searched answer, now at the palm of my hand. I met the magnitude of God in one written promise. The God, who created the heavens, the earth, and everything I see, revealed such a great depth in this passage. He holds all wisdom and expands to be a fullness that fills all-in-all. He is God, in the measures of eternity. An unattainable range. A viewpoint that is unreachable. You cannot understand Him in His richness here on earth. He has no end and He has no beginning. He is God. He is I AM. [4]

Unable to process His vast greatness, I rose abruptly. Sliding my back door open, I made my way into the house, walking through the empty hallway to my room. Shutting the door, I knelt to the floor beside my bed. Overwhelmed by who He was, I could not contain myself. My spirit cried out as the tears flowed down my face onto the carpet below. This was no ordinary prayer. Simple words were not enough. Everything inside me ached at the desire to know Him.

My heart beat quickened as I screamed out, pleading at His feet. I knelt before the Creator of all things and I told Him all about the strength I lacked. Yes, I had given my life to Jesus. I had made a decision to move forward but the battle inside was still furious. I desperately sought the fortress I would later run to often. Searching for relief, I began to pray for strength. To come to know whom He really is. Eyes squeezed tightly shut and tears rolling down my cheeks, I pleaded God to open His heart to me: a mere human. I begged Him to give me an unshakeable faith. I will never forget my petition before Him.

Hours flew by unnoticed as I remained in prayer. At 2:00 a.m., I opened my eyes and crawled into bed. Laying there, my heart continued in prayer. Though I was in bed, all of my thoughts, feelings, and attention remained focused on Jesus. The house grew still. Staring at the ceiling of my dark room, I felt a drastic shift take place in the atmosphere around me.

Prior to this, I never experienced or sought after anything supernatural. Up to this point, I have come as far as dedicating my life to God and seeking His face. I do not remember exactly when, but God gave me an understanding, all I needed was Him alone. He already prepared what I required for my life and He held my future.

As I lay there, the atmosphere began to compress, as if squeezing the air in the room. I knew this was not a dream; I was fully awake with my eyes closed. This was reality. The air grew thick around me and a weightiness pushed against my body. Physically, I trembled. My mind ran to comprehend what was happening; my immediate thoughts were I was going crazy. Those thoughts interrupted by a gentle voice, providing much needed peace. "You have dedicated your life to God. Do not be afraid." Breathlessly, I responded, "God, everything you want to do with me, just do it." As I released these words, my body swept upward in a whirlwind. To this day, I am still unsure if that was an out-of-body or in-body experience.

The surreal motion continued until someone unexpectedly took me by the hand. I froze. This new place was unfamiliar. The atmosphere fascinated me. A mixture of unique and vibrant feelings took over my body, similar to walking through an exotic garden, the air infused by the smell of fresh flowers. Vivid colors surpassed any I had ever seen, came to life around me. Every feeling within instinctively found its perfect place. The entirety of this encounter was spiritual, distinctive, and indescribable; it can only be experienced.

Regardless of my physical state, I felt peace; love, kindness, warmth, and gentleness overtook me. I could not keep my eyes closed any longer. Opening them, I clutched the hand that held me. Looking up, I saw Jesus right before me. He tenderly drew me into Himself through all the feelings that defined His nature. What I physically and mentally experienced reflected on the face of Jesus. He led me to new heights as He gently smiled and held me by the hand. I sat on His lap and He played with me as only a daddy can play with his favorite son. Something I desperately longed for. The abundance of feelings I experienced was like nothing I had ever felt before. It was only later I understood the importance of this moment. His gestures and behavior pointed to who He is. That evening, I met a presence, which became more real to me than anything else in this world.

When I was five, my parents decided to move to another city. They took the motorcycle to Sloviansk, Donetsk Oblast, searching for a new home for us. One August day, we waved them goodbye not knowing this was the last time we would see our father. As soon as they were out of sight, I ran outside to play, accidentally throwing a rock thru the window, shattering the fragile glass. I knew I would be in trouble when my parents returned.

As the day turned into evening, a telegram of devastating proportion reached us. Our parents were in a catastrophic accident. No one survived. Panic gripped us. How could our parents no longer be alive?! There were seven kids in the family, four girls and three boys. By birth, I was the fifth child and a few months shy of my sixth birthday. How could this be true? Our cries of disbelief and fear filled the house. My little body shook as tears cascaded down my face. *"God! Bring my dad back to life. Let him punish me for the broken window! I would rather have him punish me than be gone forever. Please… Bring him back home,"* I pleaded. I knew my dad, although strict, had a loving heart. I no longer cared about what kind of punishment I would receive for the broken window. I just wanted my daddy back. The thought of never seeing him again haunted me.

The motorcycle lay on top of my father's broken body, his inner organs destroyed by the collision. Bleeding, he crawled twelve meters from under the wreckage, my mother witnessing his final plea, as he lay sprawled on the ground. Groaning in pain, he prayed. His one request before God was for his children. He prayed God would protect us and show mercy to us. My father died an hour after the accident.

It was the longest night I could remember. Word finally reached us; our mother survived, but lay in critical condition. Her injuries extensive, she hung on for her life. She had flown off the motorcycle in the accident. Our prayers were not simple. We screamed to heaven, begging God for a miracle! Supernaturally, God returned her to us and breathed life back into her body. Although doctors had originally pronounced her dead, God gave her a second chance. A second chance to be the greatest influence on our lives.

The burial left me fatherless. I never experienced the full capacity of a fathers love. No one passed it down to me. My life held a variety of moments, circumstances, and seasons through which I walked alone. I had no father to guide me. I still remember watching the interaction of other fathers with their children. All the boys in my neighborhood had dads who invested into their lives. I enjoyed watching the fathers helping their kids. Each dad was like a rock and their sons leaned on them for support. I found comfort watching my friends, there was no jealousy or hurt. I was happy for them but understood my life would never be like theirs. I would never have a father.

My encounter with Jesus carried ultimate significance for this very reason. The way He took my hands and played with them demonstrated the relationship between a father and his son. When He placed me on His knees, I cupped His face with my hands. That simple gesture left a lifelong imprint on my heart, Jesus passed along the love of a real father. Only God knows the power of love. Every bit of the encounter with my Creator was intense. A single moment was enough to transfer His love into my heart. It flowed into me like the purest waterfall. I inhaled every bit of it. This same love drives me to live radically to this day. It did not occur me until later; words cannot express God's love. So radical and complex, only an experience can truly embody the fullness of this love. It is personal and uniquely tailored for each individual. In order to experience the magnitude of His love, you need to touch His being and His very nature. Love is who He is.

My heavenly Father knew a time would come when the doors to all nations would open for me. I would step into my calling realizing who I was and the purpose for my life. Realization for the reason of my existence in the physical realm, revealed. He had ordained my destiny before He created the world. God knew I would need love to fulfill His will. Carrying the message of the Kingdom into every continent requires a huge amount of the Father's love. In fact, the only way to serve people, with any gift, is through genuine love. The necessity of becoming full of love is so much greater than I can explain. All things are built on love; it is the foundation from where I do all things.

While I held the face of Jesus, He began to breathe into me. This took some time although I cannot say exactly how long. In this place, time moved in a completely different manner. As Jesus breathed into me, powerful sensations electrified my body. It was as if a mixture of oil and fire coursed through me. I heard the words of Jesus as He spoke,

"A time will come and you will go to the ends of the earth. You will serve them with what I have given you." He proceeded by explaining, He will strengthen His people and they would take action in the end times. The church would prepare the way for the second coming of Christ. Jesus told me His bride would be glorious, anointed, strong, and ablaze to fulfill her purpose as an Ecclesia; the Church of Christ would become magnificent. It would reach a position where it would confidently say, "Come, Lord."

As I sat on the lap of Jesus, I was fascinated that I did not ask Him for anything in terms of glory or money. I did not even think to ask Him for help out of my mess. There was just one thought on my mind and the words flew out of my mouth before I could stop myself, "Jesus, return Natasha to me." My bride-to-be who had hurled her engagement ring in my face and told me we would never be together. After I betrayed her, she had firmly declared she would never build her life with a person who so easily lied to her. The sound of these words put a smile on the face of Jesus. Nodding His head, He responded, "There will come a time and I will do it. You will give me all the glory for it. She belongs to you. I allowed these situations to happen. I allowed everything to fall apart so I could knock on your door. I did it to change your heart. Do not be afraid. Even if someone will want to marry her, he will be unsuccessful. She belongs to you. I arranged this."

When He said this, Jesus took me by the hands and threw me up in the air. I opened my eyes and found myself back in my room. The clock in front of me shone bright, four in the morning. I could not sleep after the encounter. Getting out of bed, I prepared for the day. That morning was a colossal turning point in my life, the beginning of drastic changes. God became more real to me than the reality of life itself.

Continuing with my day, I could not stay silent. Nothing could keep me quiet! Wherever my foot stepped, joy followed. It did not matter if I was in a store, the gym, or even a gas station. I told everyone I had encountered Jesus! He was real! He was God! Life with Him was not just a fictitious novel or some religious ritual. He was more real than the air we breathe! I preached Jesus everywhere and shared of His love with everyone who would listen. That day, every person, creature, or animal that crossed my path heard of my encounter with God. An invitation to receive Jesus extended to anyone who wondered how an experience like this could happen. I encouraged them to receive Jesus into their hearts and assured them that He could do the same with them. If they could just experience His love, their life would forever change!

As you read these words, I breathe Him in, experiencing His vastness in everything around me. God is not a religion. He is not a story or a fairytale. God is a real being. Jesus is reality and His presence is so much greater than anything around us. One encounter with the Creator forever changed me. His love, eternally imprinted in my mind. He is my loving Father and the source of life. This knowledge keeps me standing to this day. God become the daddy I run towards, regardless of circumstances. He alone can understand me and hold me. No biological father could ever bless me the way my spiritual Father does. My encounter with Him etched on my heart like a tattoo. In an instant, God had become my Father.

This is not just a depiction of my biography or journey for the sake of storytelling. Using my testimony, I want to walk you through the process of renewing the mind in a practical way. I want to show you how victory can occur in our minds.

Your mindset will determine your system of belief. This in turn will direct your words. Your words will then shape your future. Words hold power. I want my biography, experiences, and spiritual revelation to help you achieve a renewed mindset. Things will only begin to change with the transformation of your mindset. A renewed mind allows you to understand the will of God and shows you His ideal plan. He created His original ideas for your life before your life began.

Your destiny is set within a specific frame of time, a particular era on this earth. Many people existed before you and, if God so wills, there will be generations that come after you. Your existence is set in the most optimal range of time in order for you to live out your God-given purpose. God did not make a mistake when He destined your birth exactly when and where you are. He ordained it on a spiritual calendar, determining your fate long before you took your first breath.

God formed you and He knows you. He wrote out all your days when not even one had taken place in the visible world. Only a renewed mind will permit you to see your life through God's vision. That is what it means to have the mindset of God. His plan is an original blueprint and it is good, pleasing, and perfect.

God knows you hold an answer for your generation and that is why he placed you exactly where you are. He knows the time you live in and He put something in you that people are searching for. This generation needs you.

Whether or not you live out your divine destiny is completely up to you. The only way to accomplish this is by renewing your mind. I hope and pray the Holy Spirit will transform your way of thinking and steer you towards your destiny through my life story.

CHAPTER THREE

CONFRONTATION

The fulfillment of God's calling for your life does not occur overnight, it is an exciting journey walked in order to reach your glorious destiny. My biography is an intriguing story, which will bring God's truth to life. It will enlighten you. This is a chance to see yourself through the eyes of God. The encounter with Jesus was greater than anything I had ever experienced.

The spiritual world was no longer just a tale for me. It had become more real than anything in the physical world. In an instant, I understood this world has no beginning and no end. It has no boundaries. One moment in this place overturned my understanding completely.

No words or books in this physical world can ever explain God's magnitude. The human mind cannot fully comprehend it because there is no limit to His vast persona. The One who reigns forever is immeasurable. His enormity exceeds the range of eternity because He has no end. He has no birth date nor will He ever die. Eternity is in Him. God is the fullness that fills everything. He is the beginning and the end. The light, which contains no darkness. The brilliance of God began to take over my mind. All I wanted was more of

Him. One experience was not enough; I was hungry to know Him more.

I made a decision to visit my fiancée at work and tell her about my unforgettable meeting with Jesus. Driven by the promise He already made, I was certain Natasha would be mine. After all, Jesus told me He predestined her for me. Full of courage, I was prepared to explain I had no desire to return to my old lifestyle. I somehow convinced myself this would all happen instantaneously. I assumed she would suddenly forgive me and we would resume wedding preparations immediately.

Standing tall and proper, I clenched a beautiful bouquet of flowers and patiently waited for her to appear. Minutes felt like eternity until she finally walked to where I stood. As soon as I saw her, words poured out of my mouth. I talked on and on how I had changed, making sure to mention God was leading me to the nations. Full of God's energy, I radiated happiness as I spoke, expecting her to feel the same. The next moment shocked me. Her cold gaze met mine as her words pierced straight through my heart, "Andrey, I said we would never be together." My world collapsed before me as if the floor beneath me gave way. With a flip of her hair, she disappeared, leaving me in disbelief.

A million thoughts sprang to mind, all wrestling for my attention. I had no idea how to proceed. Turning to leave, I heard the malicious chuckle of the devil. He laughed at me hysterically as he hurled insults at my soul, "Where is your God now? Where is the God who promised you that she will be yours?" All hell broke loose. Everything turned against me. With my head lowered and chin tucked against my chest, I walked back to my car on the verge of defeat, devastated and full of bitterness.

Flinging the bouquet against the seat, the atmosphere in the car became suffocating. A calm voice interfered my cynicism and calmed my soul. "Do not be afraid. She will be yours. I promised you." I gripped onto this promise as if my life depended on it; it was the only thought providing me any relief. In that moment, I received a revelation. When all the situations in your life are against you, when the words you hear are nothing you expected, you need to hold tightly to one thing, the spoken word of God. The one foundation that will always remain solid. As it is written, "Man shall not live by bread alone, but by every word that proceeds from the mouth of God." [5] As I took each of my thoughts captive, I grew stronger. The voice of God within me gave me fresh hope. "Do not be afraid Andrey, she will be yours." No matter what situation came my way, I no longer cared about the lies the devil endeavored to pitch into my mind.

If there is one truth, I learned during this unending battle, it is this: the devil is the father of all lies. The original meaning of the word *father* refers to a *source*. God is the *source* of life. The devil is the *source* of lies. Falsehood originates from the devil; all untruth is his nature. The greatest tactic the devil uses is withholding the truth from humanity. Using various methods and weapons, he forces people to focus on the visible realm. He does everything he can to get people to believe in their circumstances.

To believe in God's truth, you must see beyond the physical. His truth, only seen through spiritual eyes and revealed through revelation and enlightenment. When you try to discern the truth, a battle of two worlds breaks out; a rivalry of two kingdoms emerge. The devil will always steer you towards believing your current situation is your reality. There is, however, a huge difference between your reality and the truth. Reality is simply what your physical eyes can see. When you ask God to enlighten your understanding of His will, truth is unveiled. He will show you the situation from His perspective because He wants you to live differently.

When problems arise, the devil uses the physical realm to make you believe facts, or surface level setbacks, are truth. For example, if a tumor is in your body, the pain you feel is on a physical level. The doctor will refer you to a specialist who will confirm the existence of the tumor. The devil will manipulate you in believing the reality of your situation and the unlikelihood of change. Using the words of the doctor, he will influence you in believing things his way. This is an outright lie. When you allow your thoughts to follow this trajectory, they fight against you. The facts do not line up with God's truth. God steps in when we have exhausted all other possibilities. We automatically develop feelings from these facts because we view them in a particular way. This viewpoint gives birth to the wrong reaction. We begin to act a certain way and often find ourselves in unforeseen dead ends. Think of it this way instead; the doctor told you the reality but not the truth. The truth is, two thousand years ago, Jesus took every sickness and disease upon Himself. His body received every strike and blow so you could proclaim healing over your body today.

We need to stop from simply hearing the facts and then accepting them. Instead, we must bring every fact into the light of God's truth and examine it. This is the only kind of truth that will transform our thinking. A transformed mentality will change the direction of our lives.

Words of my fiancé were brimming with emotions. The reality in her eyes was she did not want to build her life with me. Thankfully, that was not the truth. God had a plan to carry out His desires. The taunts of Satan continued as I drove home. He shrieked the false reality of my situation, attempting to sway me into believing Jesus had failed. I remembered my encounter with Jesus again. His gentle words of assurance replayed in my mind. Natasha would be mine. Despite what I had seen and heard from her, my heart filled with hope. I gripped onto the words of Jesus; it was all I had to live by. As Jesus said, "Man shall not live by bread alone, but by every word of God."[6]

That evening, as I began to read the Bible, scriptures vividly came to life as I flipped through the pages. Paul writes that He who lives inside of us is able to do significantly more than what we ask or think of.[7] The book of James also reminded me that faith without works is dead. [8] I closed the Bible and reflected on these passages. Kneeling before God, my only request was for His guidance. I was in desperate need for Him to show me what to do next. Suddenly, an idea came to mind; deliver flowers to your fiancé every day. I hesitated to accept this thought because my finances were limited, every dollar I had mattered. The problems in my life were still very real, I was dealing with many difficult situations, and I still did not have a job. Looking back, I realized God always came through when I chose to obey His voice. Daily flower deliveries it was.

The ripple effect of my obedience pleasantly surprised me. The phone began to ring. Doors began to open. Friends offered jobs and I began to work and earn money. No one knew about the decision I had made, yet relatives and friends blessed me financially. I could now afford to buy daily flowers for Natasha. After praying every night, I drove to the store to make my purchase, becoming a regular customer. Each morning, at 3:00 a.m., I delivered the bouquet to my fiancé's doorstep. This routine lasted an entire month. To my amazement, God always provided the exact amount of money I needed to acquire the flowers.

A month later, as I was playing my guitar before a church service, a song began to flow out of my heart. I stood captivated by the power of Jesus' blood. Several minutes passed and I opened my eyes in time to see Natasha walk through the back doors. There stood my bride. She was not supposed to be there, she was heading to a completely different direction for a family function in the church. A familiar voice it drew her to the auditorium where I was. The Holy Spirit came on her and she stopped. Standing there in front of me, she heard every word I sang.

That night, after so much time apart, we finally found ourselves in normal conversation. We listened and heard each other. God proved to be faithful. His words were true. Fast-forward a month; July 27, 2002, the pastor officiated our wedding as music filled the air and guests showered us with flowers. I finally married the love of my life.

CHAPTER FOUR

RESTORATION

Natasha and I decided to commit ourselves to serving God after getting married. We did not know how life would play out but our greatest desire was to seek the face of God. Like children before their father, we stood with open hearts. We longed for Him to direct us, to guide our family through His predestined plans.

When I initially met Jesus, I had not asked for glory, power, money, or wisdom. However, once God changed my mentality, He blessed me with all of those things and more. My only request, during the encounter, was to return my fiancé back to me. I had asked Him for the greatest treasure. She is exactly what I needed in my life, the perfect mate. Together, we strived to reach our destiny and fulfill God's desires.

Throughout my time in ministry, I met a wide range of people. Many of them openly shared their heart with me. In deep pain, married men shared how they were unable to prosper in life and failed to reach their God-given destiny. There was one reason, their wives did not help or encourage them. Hearing the stories of these people and observing the life of many others, I began to understand the blessing over my life. Through every season, I saw that asking God to place Natasha by my side was the perfect choice. It was a privilege to do life with the closest, dearest, and most wonderful person. It has been a joy and honor to discover God's will for our lives together.

During one of my devotionals, I discovered a powerful passage in Genesis. When God created Adam, the first man, He created him to rule. He created man to have dominion over the earth, "Then God said, 'Let Us make man in Our image, according to Our likeness; let them have dominion over the fish of the sea, over the birds of the air, and over the cattle, over all the earth and over every creeping thing that creeps on the earth." [9] Throughout different Bible passages, we find God gave the earth to the sons of men. In Psalm, David writes, "The heaven, *even* the heavens, *are* the Lord's; But the earth He has given to the children of men." [10] He created the earth for us to rule. When God said, "Let them have dominion", the word *them* refers to a person. This includes you and me.

In the beginning, God placed the person in the Garden of Eden. They were to rule from this place. The word *Eden* translates to open heaven. In other words, this is a place or environment where the presence of God dwells. God placed the person into His presence for him to rule from God's nature. He did not create the person and instruct him to love. Nor did God create a person and tell him to just glorify and worship Him. Although all of these things are factors, the primary instruction God assigned man is to rule over the earth. Allow me to elaborate on this important concept. God is interested in the entire earth. Everything filling the earth is His. His purpose for creating humankind is to bring His Kingdom to earth. After carefully examining God's intentions and His will throughout the Word, I was astonished to find that each person has a calling to lead. We are destined to rule on the territory of our calling.

In the book of Genesis, God created man in His image and placed him on earth. He gave Adam work prior to giving him a helper.[9] Before Adam received a job, God placed him into His presence or *Eden.* The first assignment given by God to Adam was to rule. Adam was the first person created and in him was the seed of all humanity. This job was the purpose for his life. God gave it to Adam who represented all humanity and all who would come after him. God gave humankind the right to rule and have dominion over the earth. In the face of Adam, God saw every other person who would come into existence. He saw them holding the ability and the power to lead and have authority on the territory of their calling. This territory is your gifting.

God created Adam with a purpose, His seed placed into him as the first human. God also placed the seed within each person. The Creator also placed a seed in you the moment you were born. That seed is the reason to your existence on this planet, which testifies to your purpose and your role to fulfill. You were born to become an answer to your generation. What happens after me is determined by whether or not I fulfill my purpose. The Bible tells us each person should serve with his or her gifting. [11] This means Jesus gives every one of us grace for a specific area. Your gifting is your *Ergon.* The word *cultivate*, original Greek work *Ergon*, refers to working. *Ergon* means to become, or to reveal yourself. If you are not accomplishing your purpose, you are not fulfilling your function in the body of Christ. This creates a malfunction in the body and produces negative effects on those who will come after you - your children and the rising generation.

There is a direct tie between your purpose and the number of days in your existence. God chose your day of arrival and your departure. You are an answer, created in your specific timeframe. Time is a resource. Everyone operates in the same twenty-four hours each day. There is no other measurement. We have one life to live, a single period of time designated for us. God has a plan by which you can live abundantly and purposefully, not merely exist. Many people live day by day; they exist but never experience true life. The territory of your calling produces real fulfillment and joy. You receive energy in the territory of your calling.

We must understand the importance of why we are here and the significance of our role. The responsibility is on us to carry out our function and purpose before we leave, it is our primary goal. Valuing our time, investing it into the right areas, and using it wisely will activate our gifting. Gradually, we must grow and become who God created us to be. Our impact and influence determines this.

God is a Spirit and each person is a spiritual being. God does not have a spirit; He is a Spirit. In the same sense, God does not have joy; He is joy. He does not have love because He is love. He does not have peace; He is peace. Man came from the Spirit of God and His nature. Although love is important, your *assigned* mission is not love. God gave humanity a task to rule on earth. It was never the final goal. Love is one of the fruits of the Spirit; it is an atmosphere, which we must carry out in our rulership. By placing man in Eden, God allowed him to rule from the position of love because he was in His presence. Man does not rule for love. God intends for you to rule in His nature. You can only do this if you remain in His presence. This kind of rulership is not dangerous; it brings no harm. Instead, it yields results and good fruit.

In order to reach your destiny, you must properly coordinate your time. This will allow you to fulfill your role by governing the earth in your designated territory. God placed Adam in the world and gave him an assignment. In Genesis, God says, "It is not good that man should be alone; I will make him a helper comparable to him".[12] Catch this next thought; first, God placed man into His presence and gave him a purpose. God already planned for Adam to have responsibility. Only after, did God decide to create a helper. The helper is essential for a family to function. The helpmate has a specific role, to collaborate and assist. Why would you need a helper if you are not doing anything?

Eve was God's created masterpiece. She came equipped with everything necessary to help Adam. Carrying strength, understanding, abilities, ideas, and support, Eve's role specifically designed to assist Adam with his mission.

Many family problems lie due to lack of vision. I often recommend young people to ask questions before they enter marriage. When a man proposes to a young woman, she must ask him about his goals for the next fifty, sixty, and seventy years. She should not only question if he loves her. It is imperative for a woman to ask questions to help her understand the man's vision; "What is your plan for life? Why do you need me? How will I be able to assist you? Who are you?" She is his helpmate and needs to understand her role in achieving the vision.

God suspended me from marrying until I understood the destiny for my life and the purpose for my existence. He was merciful towards me. With the Genesis passage revealed, I praised God for orchestrating my relationship to progress the way it did. Before God reconciled Natasha and me, she observed as I stood in the atmosphere of the

Almighty. I sang for Him, fully occupied with my appointed assignment.

After the wedding, we fully devoted ourselves to God. All of our days, years, strength, abilities, finances, and gifts would go towards fulfilling His desire for our family. The process began and continues to this day. I hope by revealing parts of my story, you will discover the potential God poured in you before birth. Remember, God destined all your days before any one of them came to be.

During this time, I began asking God for a job. The ideal position would allow me to pray often, this was my genuine request. I was sold-out and hungry for a deeper understand of God. The desire to know Him had only intensified with time. Just when I thought I was close to knowing Him, He would reveal something new, and I would realize how little I actually knew.

God has no end. He is full of riches, wisdom, strength, power, and glory. His immeasurable greatness renewed me with strength and energy to seek His face. The revelation of eternity pushed me forward. Unfortunately, many of us have stopped growing in God. We have found enjoyment in reaching ministry goals instead.

My focal point has and will continue to be the desire to know God's heart and His will for this time. His perfect will, good and pleasing, will surpass my days on earth. Opinions of others do not matter because they do not define my destiny. Many have come before me and many will come after I am gone but my burning desire is to see myself through the eyes of God. *What does God have in store for my life? How does He see me? What is His desire for this time? What is my role in this and what does He want me to accomplish?* The multitude of questions stirred my thoughts and gave me no rest. He alone could provide the answers.

Shortly after, a friend came with a job offer. The position called for a delivery driver, distributing medication. As I began the application process, I hit a snag. I had no driver's license. My reputation, from my old lifestyle, put me in bad standing with the police. The devil used my bad choices to destruct my life but I was no longer under this bondage. Before me was a new life. I knew I had to take responsibility for my actions and God would work to restore what was lost. I had to do my part and God would do the rest. An inner voice whispered to me, assuring this would greatly bless me as well as those around me. I took the risk and submitted the application. It was not long before the boss of the company called with the news; they accepted me for the position. Excited, I quickly managed to rent a van and was on the road. I promised God I would dedicate all my work hours to praying in the Holy Spirit. This proved a lot difficult to uphold since the job required me to rise before dawn each morning. By the grace of God, I spent my daily eight hours of driving in prayer.

Praying became a normal part of my life. I would come home and spend the remaining hours in scripture before my wife returned from her job. By no means is this model for everyone to follow, this is simply the way my journey began.

When Natasha came home, we headed over to the local church; the church we had decided to serve wholeheartedly. It was the same place I had surrendered my life to Jesus and I could not imagine a better place. It was my second home. We served in any way we could, dedicated to helping the church grow. People would often ask us if we argue. I always respond with, "We do not have time for that!" Our focus was to stay on track. We did not have any specific direction and there was no formula to follow. We simply had a heart for people. With everything we had, we served those around us and did our best to answer to the needs of the church. I would approach my pastor and ask where I could help; no task was too small. At one such question, he pointed me to the empty seat at the drums. I had never practiced playing but I still found my way over to them that day. It did not matter what we were doing, my wife and I were there to serve.

We came home, from church, late and my wife would go to sleep in our bedroom while I remained awake, in the living room, spending just a bit more time alone with the Holy Spirit. Only after, did I let my head hit the pillow. The alarm clock blared at three o'clock in the morning, which provided an extra half hour to pray before sunrise. To be the last one asleep and the first one awake in the house was a huge sacrifice. Those additional thirty minutes of prayer were an indication of how much I craved to know God more. I did not spend any of that time asking God for anything. My only plea was for Him to open His heart to me. To set me on the right path for the glory of His name. Isaiah writes, "Whom shall I send, and who will go for Us?" [13] Lifting my face toward heaven, I screamed, "God! Stop looking! You have found him. It's me! Take me and do what you want." I had no idea what lay ahead after praying these words. Sacrificing time became a habit. It was my daily ritual to show my hunger and thirst to know Him more. During my work hours, I prayed in Spiritual Tongues. This is a language only known to heaven. It is the most effective kind of prayer. God knows the thoughts of the Spirit. He intercedes on behalf of the saints according to the will of the Father.

As I prayed in tongues one day, I failed to see a stop sign and sped right through the intersection. I cannot justify my actions because I was at fault. An officer caught up behind me and the familiar lights signaled me to pull over. As he approached my window, I knew I was in trouble. I had no driver's license or paperwork. To make things even worse, the registration on the van was under a different name and uninsured. Sighing heavily, I lowered my head. Instead of demanding my documents, he asked me a single question. It was clear he wanted to know if I had a driver's license. Shaking my head *no,* for some reason I heard myself say, "Yes". Confused, he asked again if I had a license. Frantic, I shook my head to indicate no. Somehow, I again mumbled, "Yes". He asked me a third time. Puzzled by my response, he told me to give him whatever I had. As my hand trembled, I handed him my identification card. He headed back to his car and I slumped into my seat. When he returned, he instructed me to get out of my van and walked me to his police car. Accused of lying, reality hit me and I knew I was heading to jail. As the officer called for a tow truck, we drove to the police station. I did not know what to expect but one thing was certain, my job was on the line.

Embarrassment cast a shadow over me. How was I supposed tell this man I had met Jesus and had been completely changed when I sat behind him on the way to jail? To make matters even worse, I heard a quiet voice convict me. The Holy Spirit spoke to me, "If you had not lied but spoken the truth, you would have given me an opportunity to perform a miracle." Mortified, this was the last thing I wanted to hear.

I learned a valuable lesson that day; God cannot perform a miracle on the foundation of a lie. There is a *source* or *father* to every lie. God is the Father of eternity. He is the source of truth. The devil, however, is the father of lies. The most powerful weapon he uses to keep people from reaching their destiny is through speaking lies. If you want to see the miracles of God, learn to speak the truth. Provide this platform for God and watch as He does the rest.

Confounded by my actions, I leaned forward to apologize, "Sir, I wanted to ask you for forgiveness about lying to you." Turning his head, a smile brimmed on his face. He waited a minute before replying, "I want you to know something. Had you told me the truth, I would have let you go." My heart sank to the floor. His response made me feel even worse. God's conviction was enough. The words of the officer felt like a brick landed on my head. He continued, "I see you're a good guy. We all make mistakes so I'm going to help you. When we get to the station, I will assist you with the paperwork and do my best to let you go as soon as possible." I breathed a bit easier as hope filled my heart.

When we arrived, the officer stayed true to his words and helped ease the difficult process. Borrowing his cell phone, I called the company I worked for and asked them to send someone to recover the van and finish all my pending deliveries. The owner of the van, came to my aid and completed the deliveries for me. The next day, I was back at my job, elated.

God had stepped into my situation and resolved everything. I ended up working for the company for two years, which provided me the ability to support my family financially. Working as a driver without a driver's license is not something I will ever recommend but I had no other choice. Those two years were full of God's unforgettable miracles. He did not only restore my driver's license, but also the rest of my legal documents, which were lost. God supernaturally reestablished all the areas of my life the devil had destroyed.

CHAPTER FIVE

TRANSFIGURATION

My wife and I decided to fast every Monday. Besides ministering and helping our church, we had a burning desire for young people. In the evenings, we hosted friends in our small apartment. Together we worshiped God and prayed, seeking His face. This was just the beginning of the beginning. Every Monday morning we went to the grocery store to purchase food for the group who fellowshipped with us. Although it was our fasting day, our friends still enjoyed the meal we prepared. Dining together allowed us to share our experiences and revelations through deep conversation.

Quickly, our apartment became crowded with passionate worshipers and seekers of God. Someone would play the guitar as we sang zealously. The manager frequently came to ask us to turn off the drums. She had no idea the noise was of the voices of young people praising the Lord. To many of us, these evenings were a time for transformation. These gatherings mark the start of our shift towards destiny.

Days went by and a new week began. Keeping our Monday morning routine, I made my way to the grocery store, preparing for the evening's gathering. As the night wore on, I was surprised to see no one at our door. I could not understand how no one showed up when a week ago we had a full house. It was as if they all disappeared. I called the regulars to see if they were all right. Everyone assured me everything was fine and the absence was just a one-time deal, promising to return next Monday. I hung up the phone, telling my wife it did not matter if anyone came or not, we would still worship and seek God together. Closing our eyes, we pictured our house full of people and persisted in fervent worship.

The following Monday, I made my way to the grocery store, purchased food and waited for everyone to arrive. To my astonishment, no one showed up! I made the same phone calls and received the same excuses. The third Monday, same scenario. Confused and upset, I could not understand why God would allow this. It was as if He had shut the door in front of me and did not want us to seek Him. It was the last Monday of the month and I was curious of what the evening held.

Prior to our meeting, I locked myself in my room and prayed, intently asking God to explain what was going on. As I prayed with my face to the floor, I heard a response from Heaven, "I will teach you to serve one person so you could see the value of each individual." Hearing this in my spirit brought relief. *Whatever you desire Lord, I want to fulfill your will.*

That evening, one person showed up. This person had many problems. As they walked in, my wife and I knew we had a long night ahead of us. After praying, we began to minister and serve them. It was just before dawn when we finished. I had no time to rest. Quickly getting ready for work, I was exhausted yet my heart was satisfied. I had realized the value of one soul. In the eyes of God, every single person matters.

As I made the deliveries, I began noticing the needs of people around me. My heavenly Father gave me understanding and taught me vital life lessons. People who do not pray are unable to see the needs of those surrounding them. Their only focus is themselves. Prayer is not a few words recited before bedtime or grace prior to a meal. Prayer is a dialogue with God, a two-way street, the time you set aside to give Him your undivided attention. Without prayer, it is extremely difficult to notice those around you. People who do not pray struggle to see their own flaws and their need for God. In their mind, they are always right. When a person prays, they begin to notice areas in their personal life that require transformation. They see the need for God's grace to buff out their flaws. A deeper hunger to know God elevates us to a new level of understanding. This is where the process of transfiguration begins.

Through transfiguration, we discover deep revelations. When we accept God into our heart, we receive the entire Spiritual Being. The fullness of the Holy Spirit enters us. There can never be more of God within us because the entire divinity of the Holy Spirit is already inside of us. The only way there can be more of God is when there is less of us. The more we pray, the more we uncover what is holding us back from God's power and His nature. By cutting off the unnecessary things in our life, which are not rooted in the Heavenly Father, we make more room for God's light to shine through us. According to II Corinthians, God is a Spirit; "Now the Lord is the Spirit; and where the Spirit of the Lord *is*, there *is* liberty." [14] Freedom will come to the areas of your life in which you make room for the Holy Spirit. Let these areas be the mind, body, and soul.

We become similar to people with whom we spend time. Spending time with God and seeing His glory will begin a natural process of transformation within us by His Spirit. The moment we accept Jesus as our Savior, the Holy Spirit makes a home within us. Gradually, we open the doors of our heart and allow Him to invade and transform our life. As we dive further into Him, we no longer say we have the Holy Spirit. Instead, the Holy Spirit has us. When we allow Him to be Lord in every situation, His guidance is guaranteed. He is a teacher who equips and gives us strength. The Spirit of dominion will not remain hidden inside you because the Holy Spirit will bring it to the surface. This process takes a lifetime. The deeper your relationship with Holy Spirit, the more you will submit every part of your life to His Lordship. His management will never disappoint.

When the Holy Spirit captures us, exciting things begin to transpire. A new order of priorities intervene our prayers. We begin to not only see ourselves through the eyes of God, but also begin to notice our family. It does not matter if it is your parents and siblings or your spouse. The needs of those around us become most important. A desire to help them develops. The more we pray, the more we begin to see the brokenness in our relatives. They may seem distant, but within them lies a need for God and many unanswered questions.

As we continue in prayer, we also take note of our church. Many people blame the problems in the church on the pastor or poor leadership. Perhaps it is the lack of our involvement instead. Spend more time in prayer and you will notice the churches within your city. You will come to understand other churches are not enemies. Though their approach may be different from yours, God reveals the beauty through them as well! The body of Christ stands strong when every local church fulfills its own function. Imagine how boring this world would be if everyone was identical! Each church exists to be the light for their specific city.

Every city matters and we need to pray for the people in it. Praying for the city, you will realize the need in the state. The state will point to the country. Before long, you will go from praying about yourself to praying for the entire nation.

When the Holy Spirit changes us, He repositions our thinking and viewpoint on everything. Our mentality becomes completely transfigured. As the Kingdom of God spreads within us, our visible world changes in accordance.

My mentality had changed in this manner. Everything in my life is reordered and transformed. The power of prayer had done its work. My van continued to be a resource for me to be able to pray continually. With every passing day, I could not help but notice the needs of my family and relatives, homeless people, cashier clerks, and everyone I met. Purchasing necessities, such as food and clothing, was a practical way I served. I picked up random people on street corners and took them to wherever they needed to go. This was a great opportunity to share my testimony. I told them about who God is and the price He paid for them. Wanting to help in any way possible, I prayed for healing and deliverance and I watched as unclean spirits left, restoring health. Maybe it was because I did not give people a choice, but nearly everyone I encountered accepted Jesus Christ as their personal Savior. Numerous opportunities lay available to help the city in every corner. I did everything God entrusted me to do. In every possible way, I served the broken. Prayer never pulls us away from people. Instead, it draws us to God's heart. His heart is for His people.

One evening, after praying for one man's deliverance, I walked back to my apartment with a heaviness inside me. A battle storming within me. Realizing my insufficiency, I longed to possess a higher level of authority and anointing. I was thirsty for a downpour of strength. I knew there had to be more. When I returned, I spent some time in prayer and headed off to bed. As usual, I was back in His presence at three in the morning. My prayer that morning had been for the Holy Spirit to reveal more of what He had in store for me. I spent some time with Him and decided to get back in bed for another thirty minutes before getting ready for work. I had not yet fallen asleep and was only in bed for a few seconds, when all of a sudden I found myself watching everything from the sidelines, as if in a vision.

I did not see my body, only my wife who lay next to me. I began walking thru the front door and immediately knew I was not dreaming but having a supernatural experience. I walked right through the closed door of the apartment building. Our apartment was on the second floor and I saw the parking lot before me. I climbed down the steps and looked around. Colors of orange and pink painted the sky.

In the distance, I could make out a figure of an elderly person walking towards me. As I tried to study his face, he seemed to be thousands of years old. His white hair brushed back away from his face. Big, bushy eyebrows covered his dark eyes. As he walked toward me, his head tilted downward, his glare was a lethal stare. With every step, a venomous presence drew closer. An invisible wave washed over me, sending shivers through my body. Fear flooded me, leaving with unexplainable uneasiness. His appearance alone was recognizable. With every heavy footstep, the devil himself approached me.

The fury in his eyes, as his forehead furrowed, repulsed every cell in my body. He was the ugliest beast I had ever seen. I yelled out in utter fear and shock, "In the name of Jesus Christ, get away from me, devil!" With no reaction to my command, he marched closer. Futilely I yelled louder and louder.

I felt his putrid breath as he stood inches away from me, his eyes a bottomless pit. Hell raged inside of them. No horror movie could ever illustrate this kind of terror. Hell and its scorching wrath is much more real than we even realize. He locked his gaze with mine. Trembling as my mouth quivered as I whispered for the third time, "In the name of Jesus Christ, Satan leave me!" He had no reaction, not at all swayed by my commands.

I opened my eyes and realized I was back in my bedroom again. The chilling atmosphere filled every corner of the room. I looked at the clock, four in the morning. Then, God spoke to me, "Multiply your fasting days because you are not ready to battle with the demonic world. I will begin to teach you and open the mysteries of the Spiritual World. I will teach your hands to make war so you can destroy the work of the devil but you need to multiply your prayer and fasting."

This experience halted my deliverance prayers for a while. Every week, I increased my fasting by two or three days. The process of intensified prayer began. I cannot recommend everyone to do as I did. God gave me instructions and I followed them. This was only something I could do by the grace He gave me. Educating yourself on how to properly enter and exit a fast is very important. There were times when I lost my stance, not knowing if I was fasting or not. The weekly dedication to prayer and fasting lasted an entire year.

One night, during that year, I had an interesting dream. I dreamt I saw the face of an 18-year-old girl. After watching her behavior and facial gestures, I prayed and witnessed as two demons left her body. Seeing this, I prayed more fervently. This caused the demons to collide with each other and completely obliterate themselves. When I awoke, I reflected on the dream. I understood I was being led into the ministry of deliverance. God showed me what takes place in the Spiritual World.

A few weeks later, a young girl walked into our apartment on a Monday evening. I could not figure out how I knew her. She seemed so familiar. When everyone had gathered for our evening fellowship, we began to sing words of praise and worship. By this time, I had already ministered to many people by placing my hands on them and releasing a blessing. As we prayed, I found the girl in the crowd. Touching her shoulder, I spoke words of blessing over her and moved on. A friend found me shortly after and motioned to look back at what was happening. Turning around, I finally recognized her. God let me see the girl through His eyes. She was the one from my dream. She began to manifest and I took her to a separate room. As I prayed, God set her free.

That night, God strengthened me in authority. He gave me understanding of what occurs when I lay hands on people to pray for them. By His power, I wage war against the enemy and destroy his works.

CHAPTER SIX

HUNGER

Seeking God's face became addicting. I constantly ran to the source of living water, quenching my thirst. Our gatherings quickly outgrew our small apartment. There was not enough room to fit all the radical young people. Together, we moved to a bigger location, inside the church building. I felt the Holy Spirit prompt me to begin gathering youth from the entire city of Sacramento. By then, I already had a group of selfless people around me, ready to assist in executing this vision.

From the beginning, God always drew my attention to work with teams. He wanted me to see the world through the eyes of His Kingdom. He directed me to help young people realize their gifting and step into their calling. God did not want me to be selfish and only bring my potential to life. He instructed me to encourage those around me to become a part of God's movement. You too have God's potential within you. He has empowered you to serve and expand His Kingdom through the abilities, skills, and gifts you were born with. I learned a powerful life principle; if you want to run quickly, run by yourself. If you want to run far, run with a team. I had no idea the tug to help people was part of a God-given ability to lead greatly. He was my teacher and taught me about authority, dominion, and management.

Shortly, the large group of youth surrounding began to fulfill their proper function. Together, we began to create history. God pushed me forward to serve in the city we lived. As we marked our calendars for the first city service, marketing went into full force. Members of the team played their part to make sure everything ran smoothly. The Holy Spirit told me these services needed to occur monthly. We obeyed, holding the service on the last Sunday of every month. The direction of the Holy Spirit was very clear. He spoke further saying a seven-day fast and prayer, as a team, was vital before the event. Our team did it all. Besides the visible work and preparation of design, media, music, and home group leadership, we set fasting days and prayed.

From the very first service, the sanctuary overflowed with people. News spread rapidly and young people gathered from all over. I could not deny the Grace of God on this ministry. Many leaders and pastors heard and saw the powerful move of God. A book cannot fit the miracles and movement of God that took place during those youth services. The sanctuary, which fit 600 people, was at capacity, leaving people standing in the parking lot. It was indisputable that a movement had begun.

Setting aside time to be alone with God became even more important. Every month, I drove to the mountains to be alone. Booking a hotel room, I stopped the busyness of the clock. Time was precious. God used a unique process to mold me as I began to know Him as my best friend. The result of my time with Him was visible in the physical realm. I endured severe spiritual pressure and resistance in my everyday life. Indescribable things happened. The raging demonic world attacked me with different methods and attempts. The demons tried everything in their power to stop me but failed. The sweet aroma of God's presence elevated me to heights unattainable on my own. Strengthened by the obstacles, I strived forward and did not look back. My lifestyle comprised of being alone with God and spending time to invest into those around me. The people in the city mattered. With the drastic growth in my ministry, I was desperate to hear directly from God about what to do next. Daily prayers were not enough.

My wife and I, along with another couple, decided to take a trip to unwind and physically relax from our busy lives. By this time, I had been ordained as a youth pastor and fully immersed in pastoral care. We wanted to be a blessing to our church and the senior pastor. Ministry took a lot of strength and a trip to Santa Cruz was exactly what we needed. Due to rapid ministry growth, I felt exhausted spiritually, physically and in morale. A vacation was long overdue.

Minutes before our departure I received a call. A young man, whom I did not know, informed me a prophet had come to town and heard about the movement of God. The prophet desperately wanted to see me. My attempts to explain I was leaving town for the weekend did not sway him. He insisted I meet with the prophet. Left without a choice, I scheduled to meet with him, in a café, before the trip.

While meeting the older man, he began prophesying. He told me the place where I headed towards held significance. God had a plan and wanted to do something. This made me apprehensive, as spiritual experiences were much too familiar to me. By now, I could recognize when the Spirit was about to speak. The voice of the Spirit has its own language. I feared what was to come since all I wanted was to get some rest in Santa Cruz. I did not look for this warning, God's prophet and His word found me. As I drove, I replayed what I had just heard. Repeatedly, I told God I was under His stewardship. He could do whatever He desired. I just wanted to fulfill His will.

It was very late when we finally arrived to our vacation home. Everyone went to bed but I could not shut my eyes. Alone in the living room, I opened the Bible. I lost track of time as hours went by. The house was calm before I made my way to the room where my wife slept.

Instantly, the atmosphere shifted. Feelings I experienced before meeting Jesus invaded the space. With every breath, the pressure constricted around my body. Everything happened in slow motion, making the spiritual more tangible. The feelings were too familiar. I knew God was about to move. Recognizing the symptoms, I prepared myself. Praying in the Spirit, I asked God to do His will. As I lay in bed, the air compressed against my body and I suddenly found myself watching from above.

Strange beings appeared before my eyes. They were not very large but their appearance was gruesome. The stench radiating from them was unbearable. These demons quickly advanced, attempting to strike me. From behind, I sensed someone shield me. This Being covered me with Himself. I could not see who He was but felt Him hovering over me, like a shield of protection. The demons attacked me, multiplying in number but fell away as quickly as they approached. They were unable to bring destruction.

Perceiving their powerlessness, they began to hiss and make abnormal sounds. The noises, disturbing. As I travel the globe today, I realize what these sounds are. In many third world countries, those who are in witchcraft and practice occult, produce the same sounds. He who stood behind me was much greater than the demons who approached me. He gave them no right to hit me. The noises they made called forth more demons, which were much bigger in size. In a few seconds, they appeared next to me. Each of them wore a shoulder strap, which defined their hierarchy in the power of the demonic world. Enraged, they attempted to destroy me. The One hovering over me blocked their way.

Realizing their inability to touch me, they bolted. The demons returned shortly thereafter clasping a dazzling object in their grimy little hands. As the object swayed, it sparkled and gleamed. Using it as a tool, the demons attempted to grab my attention and distract me. With every motion, fear gripped me in its tight snare. Unable to understand what was happening, I shut my eyes.

Slowly opening my eyes, I found myself back in the room. As the eerie atmosphere invaded, I woke my wife. She is a witness to many of my experiences and events I face are familiar to her. This encounter specifically was not a surprise since, during the drive to Santa Cruz, I had mentioned what God told me would take place. The words of the prophet held me together. Even though I did not fully comprehend what was happening, I knew God was at work. Asking my wife to pray with me, I told God just how much I did not want to see those demons again. They were the vilest creatures I had ever seen and they filled me with terror. Breathing heavily, I asked God to explain the meaning behind everything and save me from this evil. Finishing my prayer, I exhaled and closed my eyes. Instantly, I disappeared again.

I found myself in an enormous building, no walls to hold up the ceiling and the structure stretched as far as the eye could see. I was only able to see what was in front and behind me. The factory.

Once inside the building, I could not see where it ended. It stretched out with no walls or boundaries to hold it in place. The building resembled a huge factory and was full of machinery. People stood behind these machines as each one performed its own function. I saw many open positions with no one to fulfill the work they required.

Observing the scene from above, I noticed a lot of work still needing to be complete, but there was an insufficient amount of people. Because so many spots were empty, those working behind the machines yelled out for help. Lacking workers, they ran from one machine to the other and attempted to accomplish many functions and tasks with their own hands. Saddened, I knew they were not completing their own work because they were understaffed. If every position had a worker, the job would be finished with quality and in a timely manner. Huffing, these people ran from one post to another.

The conveyor kept on going and so much still needed to be done. My head began to spin at the need I saw before me. The space was massive; I could not grasp how many machines there were as they went on and on. Hearing the screams of the workers, my heart went out to them in sympathy. Pleading to God, I asked Him where everyone else was and why there was such a small amount of people. Why were they missing and not there to help? Turning to the right of me, I saw a wide hallway. I watched as an obese person walked back and forth. This fat individual heard the cry of the hardworking people but ignored it.

Here, God gave me knowledge of everything I saw. This large structure represented the work in His Kingdom. Very few people are truly operating in the Kingdom. Many are too busy creating their own kingdom. They use God, anointing, ministry, and the gifts of the Holy Spirit for their personal benefit. He proceeded to say, many do not seek His will. These people use God to help them accomplish their desires and grow their own ministries. The obese person symbolizes fat Christians; those constantly fed by the Word every Sunday. Ministered to, they hear the call during every service but do nothing. Pastors and ministers feed them relentlessly. These people have grown considerably overweight from all the spiritual knowledge and food they devour. Consuming the words yet doing nothing about it, they remain obese and completely ignore the call to serve God.

He went further to explain the demons from the earlier encounter. These ominous creatures released to distract people, by various methods, from understanding who God is. Many are unable to fulfill His will because they do not know the Father's heart. Sidetracked by what the world offers, they do not seek God's face in private. These distractions include daily errands, routine, and day-to-day situations. The devil is clever with his tactics as he steals their time. He captivates people with things that deem interesting, leaving no time to be alone with God and discover the intentions of His heart.

When I received this revelation, I opened my eyes and found myself in the comfort of my room again. The sun peeked through indicating morning had come. My body ached in pain. For days, after all I had seen, I could not return to my senses. This encounter began a process in which God showed me what His Kingdom is like. His will on earth is as it is in Heaven. By proclaiming the words, "Let your will be done," we submit completely to His Lordship over our lives. We are not our own. Paid for by the blood of

Jesus Christ, we are priceless. Now, we exist to glorify Him in our hearts and bodies. I began to spend more time alone with God; the Holy Spirit encouraged me not to stay silent and to share what I had seen.

Paul writes in Ephesians, "From whom the whole body, joined and knit together by what every joint supplies, according to the effective working by which every part does its share, causes growth of the body for the edifying of itself in love." [15] Every individual receives a measure of grace according to the will of God, which He placed on his or her life. In order for us to fulfill our role and function on this earth, God gives us grace. Today, how are you and I fulfilling our role as we walk this earth?

CHAPTER SEVEN

STILLNESS

One thing in life never falls behind, time. Given to us as a powerful tool, it boasts of extreme importance. The devil fully understands the power time holds. By stealing your time, he is able to distract you from fulfilling your life purpose. He endeavors to use different methods, techniques, and forms of busyness to hold you captive.

When you understand your purpose, the value of time becomes more significant. Although we are unable to regulate time, we can still learn to manage it successfully. In His infinite existence, God still chooses to trust us with managing the time He allots. Besides dominion, we receive a skillful ability for time management.

The manner in which you invest your time will determine the distance you go and how quickly you arrive at the destination God has determined. Apostle Paul expands on this by saying, "From one man he made all the nations, that they should inhabit the whole earth; and he marked out their appointed times in history and the boundaries of their lands. God did this so that they would seek him and perhaps reach out for him and find him, though he is not far from any one of us. 'For in him we live and move and have our being." [16] The Bible reveals God chose a specific time for each of us to live out our destinies. You and I are living within the boundaries of our parameter of time. I came from God. He allowed me to be born into this world in a period that heavily operates under a system of influence. The word *world,* in its original Greek language, means *cosmos.* God purposefully allowed us to live in this specific time.

In Psalm, David speaks on the importance of bearing fruit in our own timing. I am unable to live the life of a stranger because I am confined to my own frame of time. It is very possible to live the life of someone else in your own time however, it is impossible to live your own life in the frame of time someone else is given. There is an enormous difference between the two. In order for you to be able to live your own life, you must first acknowledge that time is the most valuable resource. God has entrusted us to manage it. The same twenty-four hours cycle through every day. There is never a second more or a second less to this period. Our mentality will determine the effectiveness of our time.

Joshua writes, "This Book of the Law shall not depart from your mouth, but you shall meditate in it day and night, that you may observe to do according to all that is written in it. For then you will make your way prosperous, and then you will have good success." [17] In order to possess good judgment, we must think wisely. The way we act is determined by the way we think. Our actions correlate directly with our time. Picture these three elements connected in the form of a knot. As you dig deeper into the value of time, you begin to see your existence on earth, in this specific timeframe, matters. Your destiny, directly tied into the time you are living in and what you need to bring into this world, is unique and holds great value. Breaking down the importance of time and learning to manage it effectively will direct your way of thinking. The devil clearly understands this. He creates circumstances to hold you back by cleverly attempting to capture your attention. It is undeniable, time is a powerful resource we hold.

Your free will provides the opportunity to choose what occupies your time. The area you devote your time is the sphere that develops your thinking. It requires time to accomplish any goal you set. Psalm instructs us to "be still and know…" [18] Acquiring knowledge demands time investment. To understand who God is, we must do our part and learn how to stop and give our time. To *stop* refers to the system we are in. We can either continue living in the ways of the world or shift our focus to a different system, the system of government within the Kingdom of God. This requires us to stop and intentionally give our undivided attention to the eternal system of government. Making a decision between the two will ultimately answer one question; whom will you be enslaved by? There is a continual battle between two worlds. Whichever wins your attention is the one to whom you are a slave. Apostle Paul writes, "I beseech you therefore, brethren, by the mercies of God, that you present your bodies a living sacrifice, holy, acceptable to God, which is your reasonable service. And do not be conformed to this world, but be transformed by the renewing of your mind, that you may prove what is good and acceptable and perfect will of God." [19]

The two battles break out on this platform. You must make the right choice. Do not conform but be transformed by the renewal of your mind to understand God's will. To "be still and know", as the book of Psalm directs, we must look back from the place of knowledge to the path of understanding we traveled through. Standing at the finish line, we need to look back to where we began. The journey we walk through will show us we must keep from conforming to the world in order to *know*. To do this, we must present our bodies as a living sacrifice.

What then, is considered a sacrifice? If it cost you nothing, you cannot claim it as a sacrifice. Sacrifice, in the Bible, refers to the loss of a most valued treasure. Jesus Christ demonstrated the value of sacrifice. God gave everything He had for us. Had it just been one single soul needing salvation, God would still give a ransom for it. He was willing to give up the planets, stars, and all creation to save us. His goal is to pull everyone out of the system of darkness and control. In order for God to have ransomed the soul, an equal payment had to be paid. Humans are made in His image and likeness. In the beginning, each of us was created to be a daughter or a son of God. By giving His only Son, God paid the equivalent price so we could live as a Child of God once again. Through this action, He brought us back into the position of sonship. God's sacrifice was giving His only Son for everyone's salvation. It had cost God everything. It had cost God His entire Self.

Jesus came to this world with a specific amount of time. He presented His body as a living sacrifice in this timeframe. While reading this book, coming to understand the need to give your body as a living sacrifice is fundamental. You may be wondering why we must be a living sacrifice or questioning what it even means.

Being a living sacrifice means giving up your body for the time you live in. That is, presenting your body to God's plans for your life and seeking His will, not personal ambitions and desires. It implies you will not conform to this world. To which *world* does this refer? You and I live in a certain generation. This culture has its own values, lifestyle trends, musical influence, and so on. As we carry on through our days, the visible realm should not capture our full attention. Whatever grasps all of your attention is what will take over your time. Choosing to fulfill God's will for your life and not conform to this world will lead you to your destiny. His will encompasses your calling, role, and function on earth. In order to understand your assignment and this will, a different world needs to grab your attention. By investing time into a new world, you begin to understand the mean of life. In the Bible, Apostle Paul writes about understanding this will of God. He explains it requires you to give up your body to God for the time you are living in. You can no longer live for your selfish desires. Paul says, "Or do you not know that your body is the temple of the Holy Spirit *who is* in you, whom you have from God, and you are not your own? For you were bought at a price; therefore glorify God in your body and in your spirit, which are God's." [20] A command to glorify God in our bodies and spirits. The only path towards fulfilling this calling is through giving up our bodies and our time. Wherever you direct your body is where your time will go.

I put this into practice by setting a few days aside to be alone with God on a monthly basis. For years, I drove outside the city, locking myself in a hotel room to spend quality time with Him. This investment allowed me to understand a different realm, the Kingdom of God. There have been years where my wife and I struggled financially. With the birth of our first child, we experienced times when we had no money. On a human level, it seemed foolish to do what I did. As each month ended, it signaled my need to leave and be alone with God. I had to teach myself to disconnect from the world, to remain in His presence and come to know His will away from the busyness of the world. During the times when my family had no money, I would borrow from others to pay for my hotel room and leave the city for up to three days. People would judge me for this because, in their opinion, this was wrong and unjust towards my family, believing spending money on my child was more important. I could not explain what I knew deep within me. I understood the time I was investing would determine who I became on this earth. My future depended on this; it was an investment into my calling. The system of this world and its priorities contradicted this principle. My hunger for more propelled me to take radical measures. My desire was for God to help me see myself through His eyes. Besides the time I spent growing daily with God, I believed my monthly retreats were also a necessity.

I continue to do this today. Due to my extensive traveling schedule, I am unable to get away to be alone every month. Regardless, I use the same methods and principals while I travel. Given the opportunity to speak and serve in many nations, I continuously seek God while I stay in my hotel room. I built up this foundation for over seven years and practice in this manner to this day. Stopping the busyness of life and turning away from all the priorities of this world, I physically place my body to focus all my attention on a different world. Undefeated by the system of this world, I became a slave of God. When I first began practicing this solitude, I did not see many results. Sitting alone in the hotel room, I studied the Word of God, worshiped and praised Him. I disconnected to get connected. Prayer for me is more than just words; it is the condition of my heart.

Time set aside to be with God is an indication of your love for Him. If you love something or someone, you spend your time on it. Gifts and flowers are not everything your wife needs to know you love her. Spending time alone with her will show your love more than anything. In relationships, an investment of time is required to get to know a person. If you apply this same idea toward your relationship with God, you will come to know Him and His desires.

Only time can express your depth of love for God. Saying you love God but failing to invest your time into the relationship indicates you do not really love Him. You may love what is *godly* but not love God Himself. Time is the only indicator that God holds the greatest value in your life. He is a source you can draw from as you spend time together. Those few days, every month, brought me closer to knowing His will. The will that is good, pleasing and perfect. Understanding His heart and His desires will help define the way you see God. The transformation to become like that image is a process. This path takes you from glory to glory by the Spirit of God.

CHAPTER EIGHT

FIGHT

I had only one intention when leaving the city every month, to disconnect from the daily busyness and be alone with God. The daily hassles of life steal our time. This was my way to stop the clock and come to know the will of God. Time away provided a leeway for edifying my mind. During these saturated moments, God revealed the treasures of His Kingdom.

Using the system of the world, the devil attempts to hold you back from coming to know the truth, which will set you free. This system keeps you from understanding the real destiny God has for you. Your destiny contains the meaning of your life, your time, and your existence. When you realize your purpose, everything within and around you attains new meaning and intent.

Once I stepped out of the daily routine, the renewal of my mind brought clarity allowing me to dedicate time to know God and His ways. I chose not to conform to the rhythm of the world. Because of this, a new perspective overtook my mentality, not something familiar to me.

Two types of intentions exist. The first of these are God's intentions. They are exact, eternal, and were within Him prior to the creation of earth. Before you came to be in the visible world, your spirit connected with God. Jeremiah 29:11 says, "For I know the thoughts that I think toward you, says the Lord, thoughts of peace and not of evil, to give you a future and a hope." [22] God spoke these words to Jeremiah from eternity. He has intentions, desires, and a will for your life. As we go deeper, a more robust picture emerges before you.

God's intentions are true. Although they are real and go hand in hand with the reason you exist, we must remember God also gave us free will. We make decisions based on what we value. Knowing this, the devil's target is to create circumstances in the visible world that entice us. The things that draw our attention define our value system. Those of greatest value to us become the focal point of where we invest our time.

The devil has a mind of his own, which is the second set of intentions. His intentions clearly outlined in the book of John, "The thief does not come except to steal, and to kill, and to destroy." [22] This clever fool knows if he finds a way to steal your time he will be able to kill your calling. The devil uses the value system of the world and numerous visible methods to accomplish this. He knows by doing so, he can destroy the true meaning of your life. An epic war fights for your calling. A battle to withhold you from knowing your destiny. Remember, you must be still and know. [18]

Gaining knowledge takes time. The area you choose to invest your time will determine what knowledge you possess. Picture what God said to Jeremiah, "Before I formed you in the womb I knew you; before you were born I sanctified you; I ordained you a prophet to the nations." [24] Jeremiah was ordained to be a gift for his generation and placed into his time for a specific function. In this verse, God tells him He knew him and gave meaning to his existence before he took his first breath. King David also testifies of this, "For You formed my inward parts; You covered me in my mother's womb." [25] He goes on, "Your eyes saw my substance, being yet unformed. And in Your book they all were written; the days fashioned for me, when as yet there were none of them." [26] Even though we are formed in the womb of a woman, God sends us into the world to fulfill our role.

Born into the world, the enemy pushes us into a completely different system of government. The main goal of this system is to hold us from our calling. The devil accomplishes this by creating a false system of values and by diverting our attention using the temporary things of this time. Pulled away from what is truly important, he shoves us toward things that hold no eternal value. Tied up in the busyness of this system, people have no time to stop. They are unable to give up their body as a living sacrifice and come to know the will of God by the renewal of their mind. There is simply no time for their mind to transform by the Kingdom of God, seeing His world is out of their view.

When a child is born, it comes out alive from the inner world of the mother's womb. The Spiritual World directly influences this inner world and births the visible in the external, or physical, world. There is a distinct order of birth. First, a person originates from the spiritual world, directly from God. Followed by the formation of the person in the inner world, the seed of God makes its way into the womb. Once inside, the embryo takes shape, followed by the fetus. Only after this does birth take place.

The process through which a baby develops is a spiritual principle in all aspects. Any idea, which comes in the form of thoughts, derives from the spiritual world. The spiritual world affects the inner world, which are our thoughts. The inner world of thoughts then creates the visible world. Everything intertwines and produces results.

Anything seen in the world was once someone's idea. Prior to conception, the idea must go through a birthing process. A person is viewed as valuable or purposeful once they execute an idea. Everything visible did not just appear out of nowhere, its arrival came with a purpose. For example, a phone, chair, bed, or vehicle, came to be from an idea in someone's head who then brought the thought into reality, which now serves a purpose.

In the same way, a person springs from the spiritual realm into the inner world of the mother's womb. After conception, they are born into the physical world for a purpose. This process is extraordinary. When a baby enters the visible world, it encounters the value system of this world. This is their span. A temporary space in which they are raised.

Today, the devil uses the system of this world to occupy us with busyness. He works to fill the mind with temporary values of little importance. To imprison our attention with materialism. This is exactly what God showed me, in the spirit, while I was staying in Santa Cruz. I was able to see how the Spiritual World operates to capture a person's attention. It is unquestionable that the values of the world can tempt us. By capturing our focus, these values can absorb all our time, leaving us with no time to stop the clock and come to know God. How can you see yourself through the eyes of God if you never set aside time to be with Him? You will never realize your destiny if you do not speak with the One who created it.

The environmental impact on a baby influences their inner formation. Their exposure to the things they see, hear, feel, and experience form their way of thinking. God's viewpoint directs us to the truth. The world also presents its own perception of things. The Bible says, "Now we have received, not the spirit of the world, but the Spirit who is from God, that we might know the things that have been freely given to us by God." [27] The spirit of the world speaks its own language and affects the formation of the human mindset. Your mindset will eventually determine your priorities and value system.

The devil uses the system of this world to his benefit. Through it, he influences the way this generation thinks. He draws people into caring about temporary things. By deceiving them with the priorities of life, people automatically invest their time into the unnecessary. They get distracted to a point where they have no time to be alone with God and never come to know His will.

In Luke 21, Jesus ascertains that in the end times, people will be weighed down with carousing, drunkenness, and cares of this life. [28] The enemy's fighting against the fulfillment of your calling through the cares and busyness of this life. They stand in your way so you would never discover who you really are in God. This is why Apostle Paul teaches us not to conform to this world but to present our bodies as living sacrifices. [19] We are not our own. Purchased by the blood of Jesus, we are priceless. Therefore, we should always be available for God. We need to stand under His lordship so we can bring forth fruit in our own timing.

What God revealed to me will bless you. It serves as a huge key to unlock my calling. The visible world is like a system of magnetic attraction. People who have been to outer space explain the law of gravity. This law is not the truth because it has its own limits. By flying outside of the ozone layer, we enter universal space. This space operates under a different law. An eternal law. The universe outside of planet Earth no longer operates under the law of gravity.

When I am alone with God, I invest my time into developing a close relationship with the Holy Spirit. I practice this to know the will of God. The Holy Spirit opens spiritual laws to me and exposes the battle waged for my calling. He allows me to see how the devil attempts to use the visible world, created by God, to pull me away from the purpose, for which He created me.

In the visible realm, I must complete my mission. If I do not understand this goal, I will be unproductive with my time and will not accomplish God's desires. God broke it down for me, the less time I spend with Him, the more the system of attraction will hold power over my life. The Bible describes this concept as living by the desires of the flesh, "For if you live according to the flesh you will die; but if by the Spirit you put to death the deeds of the body, you will live." [29] Living by the desires of the flesh means all of my attention is captured by the visible world and its value system. The less time I spend investing into God's world and His presence, the more my mindset and thinking are robbed. The devil will have a greater ability to withhold me from coming to know the truth. I will never be able to see myself through the eyes of God. The busyness and cares of this world are exhausting. The more time I spend in them, the more the law of gravity takes control over my life. This will result in a life spent only on fulfilling fleshly desires. We must begin to practice *stopping* in our life. By pausing your busyness and investing time to knowing who God is, you kill the law of gravity. Transferred into another world, you no longer continue living for the desires of the flesh. The world that wins your full attention is the one that enslaves you.

I was only able to come to a place of understanding by spending a great deal of time with God. He touched me with the light of truth, which descends from Heaven and enlightens the inner person. By practicing, I was able to dominate at the physical level from the spiritual world. I threw out all the things the devil used to withhold me from my destiny because I came to see I was born from the spiritual world.

My destiny and my role are in Him. I must live them out in my timeframe. Choosing not to conform to the world in my generation, I present my body and mind before God so He can form my mindset. My thinking will determine how well I complete the role for which I came to be in the visible world. After I carry it out, I will return to God's world where I will reside forever.

God is glorified greater when we bring a significant amount of fruit. His light allows us to see light. As the light spreads, darkness can no longer stay. David writes, "He teaches my hands to make war, so that my arms can bend a bow of bronze." [30] A person, created in the image and likeness of God, includes His nature and His being. Created in His likeness comes down to having similarities with who God is. We function as He does. It is important to notice when God created man, He placed the most powerful weapon into their hand. This weapon is the ability to make a choice. God entrusted His creation to make their own mistakes.

If time is considered the most valued treasure, then this makes free will the greatest weapon. When we observe the details of a weapon, made by human hands, we pay attention to its details and determine its strength accordingly. Let us consider the atomic bomb as the strongest weapon. We easily forget this bomb has a control tied to a person's choice. Prior to detonating it, the person behind it must make a choice. Therefore, choice is the most powerful weapon. It carries great strength and determines what will happen.

God has His own intentions for you. His will is for your own good and He wants to give you hope and a future. The decision-making is now in your hands. The choices you make are directly linked to your set of values. Think about what you value. Those values determine what kind of choice you make.

The devil cannot create anything. His only weapon is falsehood and he uses it to speak lies. The enemy's intentions are to steal, kill, and destroy. [31] Using the system of the world to influence our mentality, he presents lies so we make the wrong choice. By keeping us from the truth, he is able to restrict freedom and insight from breaking out. It is vital for us to see our lives through the realm of God's will!

What captures your attention determines your choice. The visible realm, and its entire governing system, is able to occupy a person to an extent where they only care about the temporary. Demonstrating the law of attraction, it sucks the person into caring about materialistic, short-term things. When the mind of a person becomes consumed with the busyness of life, to a certain extent, they begin to believe temporary values build up the main values of life.

An individual may be brought up in a community that heavily focuses on the chaos of life. Another may live in a religious environment with its own set of teaching. This forms the mentality of the person and completely influences their subconscious. The form of teaching one accepts and lives by exhibits when the individual presents their body and time to obey a specific set of rules or boundaries. The image or spirit of this world carries its teachings, culture, and influence. It also forms ones thinking with its own set of values. Any teaching, established by humans, ties in with humanly values.

The Holy Spirit has a divine form of teaching. It is the teaching of the Kingdom of God, which sculpts our mind to become like the mindset of Christ. A person must make the choice to accept this form of teaching which correlates with God's intentions. In the visible world, God's will targets the focal point of how a person becomes an answer to their community. Through the way the Kingdom of God operates, we are supposed to influence the world. Jesus said, "You are the light of the world. A city that is set on a hill cannot be hidden. Nor do they light a lamp and put it under a basket, but on a lampstand, and it gives light to all *who are* in the house. Let your light so shine before men, that they may see your good works and glorify your Father in heaven." [32] We are created for good works. I believe that while we exist in the visible world, we must form our mindset to align with the Kingdom of God. This will serve as a path by which we will bring God's word to life in the physical world. Doing so will destroy all the devil's intentions and his demonic lies.

Serving is a key through which we can influence those surrounding us. By influence, we bring forth divine values. When we edify others through God's truth, they are set free from the slavery of sin. People are influenced by our lifestyle when we live transformed, understanding God's truth in our own lives. Edification conveyed to them through this. In this way, the Kingdom of God works like yeast, leavening the entire dough.

CHAPTER NINE

CALLING

As I continued to spend time alone with God in my secret room, the Holy Spirit began to open my eyes and show me a panorama of God's intentions. A unique process begins when God saves you. After salvation, He transforms your thinking. This greatly affects your life and releases you to accomplish your specific assignment. Jesus spoke to His disciples saying, "Therefore pray the Lord of the harvest to send out laborers into His harvest." [33] Jesus is the Lord of the harvest and holds everything under His supremacy. He is the one who must release you to do the work He set aside for you. The work laid out for you is in His will and a part of His plan. You were born into the world for this very work. His task for you is beyond any abilities you currently have. It is much bigger than you are. To complete His mission on earth, you desperately need His strength. In Matthew, Jesus called his disciples, men He designated, to himself. [34] Before releasing them to minister, He called them to abide with Him. This is an important aspect for those who truly and sincerely want to seek God's way toward their destiny. This applies to you as well if you want to complete the will of our Heavenly Father on earth. Jesus said, "My food is to do the will of Him who sent Me, and to finish His work." [35] God is preparing you for something specific He desires to be complete on earth. Only after God equips you, will He release you with His power and anointing.

I have discovered three types of callings. The first calling is internal. The second is external and the third is eternal. Each of the three influence one another. They also release one another. The spiritual world affects the inner world, which is our thoughts. The inner world creates what we eventually see in the external, or physical, world. In turn, the external world we create will determine the eternal world.

Paul writes, "And we know that all things work together for good to those who love God, to those who are the called according to *His* purpose. For whom He foreknew, He also predestined *to be* conformed to the image of His Son." [36] I believe our inner calling requires a process of transformation. We must conform to the image of God's own Son, Jesus.

The inner calling is to become like the Son of God. It is to have the nature of Jesus and His qualities. The purpose of Christianity portrays the process of becoming like Jesus. The meaning of *Christian* derives from being Christ-like. Apostle Paul writes, "My little children, for whom I labor in birth again until Christ is formed in you." [37] What meaning stands behind these words? It completely connects with what will occur externally and eternally. Inner calling requires transfiguration to become Christ-like. It also binds with what will take place in the external calling or your destiny.

Your function on earth is to complete the work of the Heavenly Father. It is extremely crucial that you complete it in the power of God as you glorify and represent Him on earth. Your inner transfiguration will determine how you will present God to those around you. The deeper the transformation, the greater the power of God will be released. His power coincides with personal transformation. God is glorified through the completion of work that is tailored for your life. The greatest level of transfiguration is to become like Christ. This is what the Bible teaches us and Apostle Paul emphasizes this point, "To the measure of the stature of the fullness of Christ." [38]

It is always a possibility to meet an unbeliever on the territory of your calling. This is where you have influence. The person you meet must be exposed to the God you represent before anything else. Depending on how you present God will determine the decision they make. Will they choose to receive Him into their life and serve Him or walk away? Every Christian has an enormous responsibility. Everything stems from here and is the main element of your area of influence. When meeting you, unbelievers care very little about the role you play. To them, it does not matter if you are an apostle, evangelist, musician, artist, or anyone else. The question to answer is will they come in contact with the nature of God when they meet you? Do you represent God in your life? Can people see God in you?

The process of inner transformation is significant as well as intricate. The moment you enter your Garden of Gethsemane, you die to yourself. You can do this only through encountering God. The words of John the Baptist explain this, "He must increase, but I *must* decrease." [39] Many people become lost in this stage of the process. Presenting our lives as a living sacrifice is a choice we must make. Making this choice will help us not conform to the ways of the world. It all begins with inner transfiguration and will end once we enter eternity. This process directly connects with the knowledge and understanding of who God is. The word *understanding* means connection. Connecting with God requires us to meet with Him regularly. Paul outlines this in Corinthians, "But he who is joined to the Lord is one spirit *with Him.*" [40] Our destiny derives from being with Him. This brings us to our external calling.

The fulfillment of your destiny directly correlates with your obedience to God. It will also determine your eternal reward. The measure you choose to obey God on earth will define your level of glory in Heaven, which is eternal. God called us to live eternally. In eternity, we will not all have equal glory. In fact, there will be various levels of glory. Our obedience to what God desires for us on earth is of paramount importance. Staying connected with the Holy Spirit will help us hear His voice and better understand His expectations for our lives. Notice the intertwined connection. It is impossible to pull one piece away from the other. A three-folded knot, functioning together to complete its role.

In Colossians Apostle Paul writes, "For this reason we also, since the day we heard it, do not cease to pray for you, and to ask that you may be filled with the knowledge of His will in all wisdom and spiritual understanding." [41] A significant detail needs to be uncovered, the need for us to be filled with wisdom and the spiritual understanding of God. This applies to every reader regardless of what condition you are in as you hold this book in your hands. It does not matter if you are currently serving or not. Perhaps you recently accepted Jesus Christ or do not know of God yet. All this aside, you must know there is something greater. You were born for greatness. God has written an immense destiny, which will add incredible meaning to your life.

Paul continues by writing, "That you may walk worthy of the Lord, fully pleasing *Him,* being fruitful in every good work and increasing in the knowledge of God." [42] In verse nine, his instruction is to be filled with the knowledge of God's will. The will of God is His desires, intentions, and thoughts. In verse ten, Paul completes the message by stating the need for us to increase in the knowledge of *who* God is. It is impossible to know the will of God and yet not grow in the knowledge of who He is as an individual being. It is only through a personal connection we can understand His desires. God Himself stirs within us His desires and leads us to action.

Because of this, Apostle Paul writes his experience in the book of Colossians, "That you may walk worthy of the Lord, fully pleasing *Him,* being fruitful in every good work and increasing in the knowledge of God." [42] How can we fully please Him in everything? It is only through obedience. When we hear the voice of God, we understand what we must do, when we must complete it, and how to accomplish it. Hearing and obeying God's voice pleases Him. The inner calling influences the external calling.

To go deeper, the inner calling branches out into the external calling through the process of transformation. Becoming more like God, through our connection with the Spirit of God, unlocks a door for us to deeper understand His desires. He pulls us from our internal world of thoughts into external calling.

No one knows what is of God except for the Spirit of God. Scripture says, "As His divine power has given to us all things that *pertain* to life and godliness, through the knowledge of Him who called us by glory and virtue." [43] It is through the knowledge of who He is we come to know what is given to us by God. Understanding comes from revelation. Revelation stems from relationship. A relationship's foundation is communication and communication requires time. Have you noticed how time is an indicator of love? It is what determines the depth of a relationship. Investing time to communicate with the Holy Spirit develops a personal relationship. God opened this spiritual view and revealed it to me. The Word states, many times, that God opens up to us through His Holy Spirit. The Spirit dwells in the deepest of depths. He releases a revelation when there is a relationship, which opens a door to understanding. Revelation connects you with the nature of God. As a result, knowledge naturally becomes a part of you. Through this process, God uniquely pulls us from the internal, which is private, to the external, which is public.

The Bible warns us; all acts done in secret will become known. [44] Therefore, the personal relationship you have with God, in your hiding place, will gradually be revealed in the open. Systematically, everything God speaks to us becomes complete. In Psalm, David writes, "He leads me in the paths of righteousness for His name's sake." [45] To be led, you must first hear His voice. Obeying God's command will glorify His name. He will guide you through the path He has predestined for your life.

It did not matter how much time I spent at work praying in the Spirit. I would come home, lock myself away to pray and read the Bible for at least another couple of hours. In my prayers, I asked God to allow me to hear His voice even more. I wanted to understand His voice more clearly and constantly asked Him to speak to me. One day, I returned home from work with a longing to hear His voice like never before. A sudden thought interrupted my yearning, *"Get up, leave the room, and transfer the wet clothes from the washer into the dryer."* The apartment complex, my wife and I lived in, had a separate laundry room for everyone to share outside of our unit. In order to reach the laundry machines, I had to walk across the entire property. When I came home from work that day, I had gone over to the laundry room and loaded all of my dirty clothes into the washer. Inserting some coins into the machine, I started it and returned to my apartment to pray. It was during prayer when I received this sudden thought to go switch my load into the dryer. Thinking it was a distraction from the devil I rebuked it and continued to pray. The more I pressed into the presence of God, the more the thought to take care of my laundry echoed in my mind. Overwhelmed, I stood to my feet knowing if this thought was truly from God, then He would provide clear understanding.

I opened the main door to the apartment entrance and saw an Asian woman enter the laundromat. I instantly understood God wanted me to tell her about Him. Walking to the laundry room, I internally spoke to God, *"God, if this is truly you then allow me to understand. When I come into the room, have her speak to me first. If she does, then I will know you really want me to tell her about you"*. Stepping through the entrance, the woman turned to ask how I was doing. Realizing the divine connection, I understood this place was where I would serve her. He brought me out of my private place onto a public platform. Sharing my testimony, that evening, took all of twenty minutes. As tears rolled down her face, I asked her if she wanted to accept Jesus Christ into her heart. Nodding, she pushed her laundry basket aside and wholeheartedly accepted Jesus Christ.

After the prayer, she also asked if it would be okay to pray over her sister who was sick with cancer. Which I did not hesitate to do. It is such a privilege to bring people to Christ. I directed her to find a local church and we parted ways. Halfway back to my apartment, the same inner voice stopped me and instructed me to turn around. As I looked back into the direction of the laundromat, I saw the woman running out of the building, with a basket full of clothing, the biggest smile stretched across her joyful face. She did not seem to notice me watching her from a distance. The voice inside me asked, *"Are you happy to see this?"* Responding, all I could say was, *"Wow Jesus, Yes!"* A flood of satisfaction filled my heart. I could not deny how incredible it had been to watch the child-like joy on the face of this woman. God replied, "Oh how happy it makes me when my children listen and obey my voice. If you would obey my voice, you would witness so much of my power and glory. I would fulfill my desires and intentions on this earth."

God taught me to remain in Him. To hear His voice and obey it, discovering a new language through vision, revelation, and closeness with the Holy Spirit. We are able to hear God's voice inside of us. The spiritual language is similar to a multidimensional object, it is unable to be limited or bound to one method. Learning the lesson, what is done in private becomes known in public, I ran back to my room to thank my God. The verses from Colossians came alive within me. We can come to comprehend His will in all spiritual understanding. Walking worthy of the Lord, doing good and pleasing works is the greatest privilege.

I want to demonstrate a small example of the long process we must undergo in our lives. Ministry work for others derives from inner transfiguration. Fulfilling our calling determines the level of our reward in Heaven. God will never entrust you with something big if you are not faithful in the small. Running a worldwide ministry today, I stand in stadiums full of hundreds of thousands of people. Although now entrusted with much, I am reminded it all began from my simple, faithful steps. The small details should never be ignored. It is behind the scenes where God allows us to be victorious.

Obeying God's voice and completing exactly what He desires activates anointing in our lives. Your anointing links the work God has designated for you. The Holy Spirit reveals what kind of work that is. When God speaks to you, He leads you from the internal to the external calling. The small steps matter. Anointing will only increase when you obey Him because it serves a purpose. Luke illustrates this concept, "The Spirit of the Lord is upon Me, because He has anointed Me to preach the gospel to the poor; He has sent Me to heal the brokenhearted, to proclaim liberty to the captives and recovery of sight to the blind, to set at liberty those who are oppressed." [46]

Listening to God and receiving from Him guides you on the righteous path. The path customized and predestined for you and anointing given to activate and teach. Your obedience on earth elevates your level of glory in eternal realms. This is the reward. It is a place where you will be with Him forever.

My friend, I believe the inner calling is to become Christ-like. Through obedience, this inner calling flows into your external calling. Your God-given destiny, or external calling, will determine the level of glory you will receive in your eternal calling.

CHAPTER TEN

CHOSEN

In my years of ministry, I have seen many people dedicate themselves to serving God. This element, however, is not the most important. Dedication to God himself will determine the quality of ministry.

In reading the story of Moses, we observe a delicate process unfold. [47] This progression directly correlates with the strength of our calling. It is not only about fulfilling the duties of our calling but also accomplishing them in the strength of God. Approaching our calling in this method will bring inevitable change to the visible world.

In Exodus it says, "Now Moses was tending the flock of Jethro his father-in-law, the priest of Midian." [48] Because of his situation, Moses's intention was to serve through one action, managing the herd. Witnessing an Egyptian beating a fellow Hebrew man, Moses became infuriated and interceded. Although he desired to serve with good intentions, Moses had unfortunately intervened in his own strength. It is daunting to influence people using authority. In our lives today, we see people with seemingly right intentions and a desire to serve God. From a distance, it appears they do great works with a sincere heart. The problem is the timing is wrong. God had not yet released

Moses to fulfill His work. Feeling the need and urgency to serve, Moses relied on his own strength. As a result, he had to flee from Egypt to escape death.

As we read Moses's story, years passed and he continued to live in his father-in-law's home. Imagine the thoughts invading his mind during this time. I am sure he worried ceaselessly but the scripture does not provide details on this. It was because of his situation that Moses ran from Egypt. The Bible tells us Moses was mighty in words and deeds during this time. [49] However, in Exodus, we see he did not feel the same way about himself.

Internal changes continued to occur in the life of Moses. In an unexpected moment, his life drastically changed. This one unexpected moment is the basis of this entire book, for you to walk away, after reading the text, and never return to your old life. We all desperately need this one moment.

My trip to Israel compelled me to take a closer look at the story of Moses. "He led the flock to the back of the desert, and came to Horeb, the mountain of God." [48] As I stood, the desert stretching for miles before me, I understood Moses had to make a definitive choice to take his flock to the back of the desert. I do not know what prompted him to go farther than his normal route but I believe it was because the timing of God had come for his calling. God stirred an inner desire for him to go beyond the ordinary path. Because this passage tells us Moses went farther into the desert, we can conclude, for a certain amount of time, he had been leading his flock within a specific distance.

We can apply this verse to our own lives. By now, we may have grown comfortable with our regular life. Being in a state where we seem to know everything is a dangerous place for us, as Christians, to be. We can never go further if we live within the radius of comfort. I pray the Spirit of God will prompt you to move beyond, to go further. It is there you can truly meet the real, living God. One powerful encounter with Him will change you forever. You will never be able to return to your old way of life after it. The Bible instructs the holy to continue being holy. The righteous individual to continue living righteously. [50]

It is unsettling how many people's prayers stay within a certain scope. Perhaps you yourself have never gone further in your prayer life. Some of us have never stepped beyond a specific point in our relationship with God. Our fasting lifestyle stays within normal limits. This is our familiar zone. I want to implore you to step outside of your boundaries and move further. Be the person who willingly does far more than what is average.

As Moses approached the mountain of Horeb, an astonishing encounter took place. "The Angel of the Lord appeared to him in a flame of fire from the midst of a bush. So he looked, and behold, the bush was burning with fire, but the bush *was* not consumed. Then Moses said, 'I will now turn aside and see this great sight, why the bush does not burn.' So when the Lord saw that he turned aside to look, God called to him from the midst of the bush and said, 'Moses, Moses!' And he said, 'Here I am.' Then He said, 'Do not draw near this place. Take your sandals off your feet, for the place where you stand *is* holy ground.'" [51] What a profound moment! Through an angel, God dwelled in the midst of a burning bush. Although it stood burning, fire did not consume it. This is what drew Moses's attention. Many bushes burn in the desert but this one stood out.

There is a fundamental principle, from this story, to apply to our lives. When I fully surrendered my life to God, I received a breath of life from Jesus Himself. I experienced this kind of fire. People constantly told me that with time I would burn out and calm down. I never received those words. There was no way those negative words aligned with His will. As I spent time with God in prayer during the night, I asked Him, "God is this truly your will? For me to burn for a bit and then settle down and become like everyone else who spoke those words into my life?"

It was a bit later when the Holy Spirit answered my question. He spoke, guiding me to read the passage in Leviticus, "The fire on the altar shall be kept burning on it; it shall not be put out. And the priest shall burn wood on it every morning, and lay the burnt offering in order on it." [52] God's desire is for the offering to burn and not burn out. He also instructed me to present my body as an offering a while back. The fire still burns without consuming my offering. God continued to reveal being burned-out is not part of His will. Instead, His will is for the offering to continually burn. In fact, it is not only to keep burning but also to intensify and increase the flame even more. The level of fire completely depends on whether the priest continues to add wood. The more wood on the altar, the greater the flame of fire. God spoke to me saying every day requires me to put more wood on this altar. My relationship with God determines my flame. In order for my fire to burn constantly, I must abide in prayer and read His Word. The wood on the altar is my inner condition. Ever so lovingly, God told me He would speak from the midst of this burning fire. As we burn, it is important for God to do this.

Many years have passed since my question. I stand as a true witness today to the fact the flame of fire indeed grows bigger and does not burn out. Ministering around the world, people ask me, "How have you not burnt out?", "Where does this flame of fire come from?", "Where do you get that inner passion?" My response derives from the very words of

Apostle Paul, "Not lagging in diligence, fervent in spirit, serving the Lord." [53] In order to serve the Lord, our spirit must be a flaming fire, achieved by not falling behind in our diligence. As the new day begins, we must put wood on the altar so we can burn and hear God's voice in the midst of everything.

God speaks to Moses saying, "'I *am* the God of your father—the God of Abraham, the God of Isaac, and the God of Jacob.' And Moses hid his face, for he was afraid to look upon God. And the Lord said, 'I have surely seen the oppression of My people who *are* in Egypt, and have heard their cry because of their taskmasters, for I know their sorrows. So I have come down to deliver them out of the hand of the Egyptians, and to bring them up from that land to a good and large land, to a land flowing with milk and honey, to the place of the Canaanites and the Hittites and the Amorites and the Perizzites and the Hivites and the Jebusites. Now therefore, behold, the cry of the children of Israel has come to Me, and I have also seen the oppression with which the Egyptians oppress them. Come now, therefore, and I will send you to Pharaoh that you may bring My people, the children of Israel, out of Egypt.' But Moses said to God, 'Who *am* I that I should go to Pharaoh, and that I should bring the children of Israel out of Egypt?' So He said, 'I will certainly be with you.'" [54]

From a simple act of going further in the desert, a pivotal moment resulted in the life of Moses. Approaching the mountain of Horeb, he encountered God. As the story unfolds, we find Moses bringing God's people out of Egyptian captivity, taking them to the mountain of Horeb. Circumcision occurred there. This detail is crucial; we can never lead people to a place where we have not yet been with God. The true mark of a good leader, in ministry, is when he or she leads people to a place where they have already been with God themselves. God began to share His vision with Moses in this place. It is incredible how He revealed His desires to Moses. When we meet God, He begins to open His heart to us. Here, we come to understand His will. God acknowledged the oppression of His people; he heard their cry. He said that He knew their sorrows and He declared He had come to deliver them. [54] How extraordinary it was to hear those words from God!

Something similar often occurs with us. As believers, we may hear a specific prophetic word or the voice of God break through when we cry out to Him. God boldly speaks to us saying He has seen, heard, knows, and He is coming to the rescue. God's intentions for Moses ended up being His will for Moses's life. Shortly after, God commanded Moses to go. Many people become confused at this part of the story. God spoke to the people saying He would come because He saw and knew their struggle. God is a Spirit and He is unable to do anything on this earth without a body. He needed a human who would present itself as a sacrifice. A mind, transformed by coming to know the will of God. Eventually, God sent Moses. By coming in contact with God and His vision, Moses met his mission. By hearing the voice of God and obeying it, Moses entered his calling.

When we meet God, we encounter our own self. Something remarkable happens when we see our life through God's eyes. He knows our destiny. Through a vision, God showed Moses how He viewed him. If we do not see our life though God's eyes, people will always be the determining factor of our future. People do not see us the way God does. He carries a specific vision for our lives.

God has one vision, one body, one faith, and one baptism. We are the body of Jesus Christ, which consists of many members and functions. Our goal is to fulfill God's will on earth both individually and collectively. We must recognize God is calling us into His vision. He is the head of the body as well as the head of our life. Staying connected with the head is vital in order to think like Christ. There is power in a renewed mindset. Called into God's vision, we discover the meaning of life is found in goals and a specific type of work for every individual. This leads us onto a path toward our destiny.

When Moses met God, God told him how He viewed him. God saw Moses as the one who would deliver His people out of Egypt. For this reason Moses was born. Four hundred years prior to Moses' existence God spoke to Abraham about the deliverance of His people from Egypt. Long before the time came to be, God spoke to Abraham about Moses. He designated Moses and conceived him for this moment. Meeting God gave Moses his true purpose and set him on the path of righteousness. Through the obedience of Moses, God was able to complete His work on earth.

The reaction of Moses revealed how he viewed himself, inadequate for such a task. He viewed himself as someone very small and incapable. God's vision for his life was so much bigger. Dear reader, please know, when the Spirit of God begins to show you how He sees you, it will always be greater than what you see. His desires for your life will be much grander. Looking at ourselves, we typically find it difficult to believe God can do what He said He could do through us. Keep your focus on Him. Moses responded to God, "Who am I?" [54] He was most likely remembering the time he attempted to do something in his own strength and failed. The difference between the two attempts at action is this; the first time an opportunity arose to do something, Moses tried to do it with his own hands. His ego was in the way. Moses wanted to reveal his own strength. By the time the second call presented itself, there was nothing left of his ego. He did not view himself in any particular way. God promised this time He would be with him. All Moses had to do was set himself apart for God.

God's vision required Moses to be dedicated one hundred percent. A complete sacrifice. It was far more than ministry work. Set apart for God, Moses fully commit his life to Him. Study the radical changes in Moses's life the moment he decided to go further. All it took was a step extra than the standard radius of space he was accustomed to. Most likely, Moses knew very little about the power behind this choice. Going further will forever change your destiny and history itself. After the divine encounter, Moses never returned to his old lifestyle, all because he once walked further into the desert and met with God. A key factor to remember, for those who set themselves apart for God, bringing people out of slavery and captivity is God's will and His intention. The end goal of destiny, as a whole, is to set people free in all spheres. This includes the spiritual, mental, and physical aspect. Jesus has already done it all. Our job is to guide people from lack of knowledge into freedom. Here, they will come to know the truth and experience deliverance. As a result, people will then fulfill God's will for their life in their own territory.

God sent Moses to Pharaoh to deliver His people. Under Pharaoh's control, the people were captive and bound to slavery. For Moses to stand before the ruler, he required strength and authority. Moses was able to destroy Pharaoh's force through a different strength. "Then Moses said to God, 'Indeed, *when* I come to the children of Israel and say to them, 'The God of your fathers has sent me to you,' and they say to me, 'What *is* His name?' what shall I say to them?'

And God said to Moses, 'I AM WHO I AM.' And He said, 'Thus you shall say to the children of Israel, 'I AM has sent me to you.'" [55]

Moses asked God the most difficult question. How could God determine who He is? How can we determine what is undeterminable? God has no beginning and no end. In Him is a bottomless depth that is rich in wisdom. His strength has no boundaries. Someone the size of eternity needed to describe Himself. The author of words needed to find words to define Himself. God can only be expressed, therefore, God tells Moses, "I AM WHO I AM." [55] What a defining moment! God's essence and strength are in this name.

A name is not just a word; it is what determines the substance of what is being named. When someone calls your name, it is more than just a word. Your name justifies the core of who you are. This can carry either a positive or a negative connotation. Here is where the difference lies. Two individuals may say the name *Jesus*. For one person, as soon as that name is spoken, something begins to stir. For the other person, everything remains the same. It is not necessarily something magical about the name *Jesus*, but rather His nature behind it, which brings change.

The more we transform into the likeness of Jesus and His character, the more we begin to look like Him as His attributes grow within us. It is only then our words release His essence when we proclaim the name *Jesus*. If we do not transfigure into His image, there is no power or strength to back up the name when we speak it. If we do not transform, the spoken name will lack power.

This is why God instructs Moses to go tell His people He is *I AM*. In other words, *I AM* will go with him. Through Moses, Pharaoh would see God. Ultimately, God revealed Himself, His strength, and His majesty before Pharaoh. In order for this to take place, Moses needed to present his body, which he did, and set himself apart fully for God. Through Moses's obedience, God was able to demonstrate His core and strength before the ruler and show Pharaoh He is Lord. In the end, Pharaoh indeed saw there is a God and He is ruler over all.

CHAPTER ELEVEN

DEDICATION

Moses prophesied of the coming of Jesus Christ to the people of Israel saying, "The Lord your God will raise up for you a Prophet like me from your midst, from your brethren. Him you shall hear." [56] God the Father was speaking of Jesus. He revealed Jesus would come to destroy the authority of the devil. In this story, Pharaoh portrays the devil. Colossians confirms what Jesus accomplished stating, "Having disarmed principalities and powers, He made a public spectacle of them, triumphing over them in it." [57]

In Joshua, God speaks of who Moses was, "After the death of Moses the servant of the Lord, it came to pass that the Lord spoke to Joshua the son of Nun, Moses' assistant, saying: 'Moses My servant is dead.'" [58] In this passage, God affirms the full dedication of Moses, who completely sold-out to God alone. Serving people is an element of God achieved through him.

We see a similar devotion in Romans. Paul introduces himself as "a bondservant of Jesus Christ." This greeting serves to show Paul also set apart for God. Paul was "called *to be* an apostle, separated to the gospel of God which He promised before through His prophets in the Holy Scriptures." [59]

Reading the words of Moses, God says He will raise up the people needed among the prophets. [56] In Romans Paul writes, "Concerning His Son Jesus Christ our Lord, who was born of the seed of David according to the flesh, *and* declared *to be* the Son of God with power according to the Spirit of holiness, by the resurrection from the dead. Through Him we have received grace and apostleship for obedience to the faith among all nations for His name." [60] It is here God affirms His Son, Jesus, through the prophets. Although Jesus was born in the flesh and from the seed of David, God revealed Him as the Son of God with power according to the Spirit of holiness. In short, He was born of flesh but revealed as the Son in the Spirit. Moses was also born in the flesh from a seed. However, in a specific time, God declared Himself in power before Pharaoh through Moses, according to the Spirit of holiness. The same occurred in the life of Paul the Apostle.

We must come to understand the power of God is on the side of dedication. Holiness is composed of two aspects; meaning He set us apart *from* something and He set us apart *for* something. If I separate a cup from a dish, then the cup is set apart for me. Whenever God sanctifies anything in the Holy Scriptures, He makes it holy for Himself. By setting people apart from something, he dedicates them for Himself.

Jesus, born in the flesh from the seed of David, now revealed as the Son of God through the Spirit of holiness. God set Jesus apart for Himself. He set Jesus apart from the glory of Heaven and sent Him to earth to dedicate Himself fully to the heavenly Father. The will of the Father complete through the body of Jesus Christ on earth. The described process, through these lives, consists of many parts and is vital to understand. Through it, God releases His power.

Studying the life of Jesus, we see that in everything He was fully dependent on the Father. Jesus says, "He who has seen Me has seen the Father." [61] In another passage, He states, "For I have not spoken on My own *authority*; but the Father who sent Me gave Me a command, what I should say and what I should speak." [62] These scriptures show, through commitment, Jesus was a servant to His Father. He made a conscious decision and followed through. Scripture also confirms this, "Most assuredly, I say to you, the Son can do nothing of Himself, but what He sees the Father do; for whatever He does, the Son also does in like manner. For the Father loves the Son, and shows Him all things that He Himself does; and He will show Him greater works than these, that you may marvel." [63] The Bible reveals Jesus' complete dependence on the Father. As a Son, He is not able to do anything unless He sees His Father doing it.

To this day, God the Father reveals His intentions, desires, will, and vision. If we are not seeing our Father doing something, we begin to look at other people who are creating things around us. This is the creation from the hands of people. Jesus said He is unable to create anything from Himself but only what He sees the Father doing.

God gave humans free will. Likewise, Jesus also had the option of doing His own will while on this earth. Jesus' time spent in the Garden of Gethsemane clearly depicts this, "Do you think that I cannot now pray to My Father, and He will provide Me with more than twelve legions of angels?" [64] Exposing the human aspect, this passage reveals Jesus had a choice and could have taken a different approach. Jesus had full rights however, as the Bible says, He was obedient to the Father in everything, even to point of death through crucifixion. [65] Jesus not only set Himself apart, but also devoted Himself fully to the will of the Father. In our Flame of Fire Ministry, we speak on three main principles: full dedication to God, full sacrifice, and full obedience to the Holy Spirit. I believe this is what distinguishes true Christianity and releases the power of God.

That night in the Garden of Gethsemane, soldiers approached Jesus. Let this image sink into your mind. Holding swords and weapons, the soldiers marched in to take hold of God. Jesus had volunteered to submit to the Father. He made a choice to dedicate Himself fully to God. As the soldiers came closer, they were determined to take Him by their own strength. Jesus, in turn, did not reveal His strength to them. Instead, He revealed the power of His Father, the core of who He is. Jesus asked the men for whom they were seeking. They sought Jesus. In this moment, Jesus defined God in the same exact name as Moses was instructed to use *I AM*. "Jesus therefore, knowing all things that would come upon Him, went forward and said to them, 'Whom are you seeking?' They answered Him, 'Jesus of Nazareth.' Jesus said to them, 'I am *He*.' [66] Even here, Jesus did not reveal Himself but presented the Father. In one of His earlier prayers, Jesus said He had done everything to reveal the Father to the people. [67]

Every time Jesus heals, He reveals God as the Healer. [68] By raising the dead back to life, He shows the Father as the Resurrector. [69] When feeding the multitudes, He displays the Father as the bread that came down from Heaven. [70]

"Now when He said to them, "I am *He*," they drew back and fell to the ground." [71] Through those two authoritative words of *I AM* Jesus displays the spirit of the Father, which releases power. The same occurs in Exodus, God instructs Moses to reveal Him as *I AM* before Pharaoh, releasing power. [55] From then on, Moses walked in God's power. In the Garden of Gethsemane, everyone drew back and fell at the words Jesus released. [72] Showing His full dedication to the Father, He willingly gave Himself to the soldiers who came for him. The will of the Father was for His son to die and set His people free from slavery.

Moses was born in the flesh and through consecration, God revealed Himself in power according to the Spirit of holiness. Jesus, also born from the seed of David, in the flesh, dedicated Himself to God. The result of devotion is a downpour of God's anointing and revelation in power.

In the book of Galatians, Apostle Paul writes, "When it pleased God, who separated me from my mother's womb and called *me* through His grace, to reveal His Son in me, that I might preach Him among the Gentiles, I did not immediately confer with flesh and blood." [73] God had called Paul to Himself. Set apart for God, the apostle fully dedicated himself to God and His plan. The plan of God was to reveal His son. For a pathway for the power of the Holy Spirit to be established, Paul needed to become like Christ. Apostle Paul writes, "For I will not dare to speak of any of those things which Christ has not accomplished through me, in word and deed, to make the Gentiles obedient—in mighty signs and wonders, by the power of the Spirit of God. So that from Jerusalem and round about to Illyricum, I have fully preached the gospel of Christ." [74] The passage emphasizes God wants to reveal His Son through His people, which includes you and me. Therefore, Paul did not consult with flesh and blood. His feelings and surroundings mattered very little to him. At one point, he decided to go further into his desert where he met the living God. Apostle Paul declared himself as a servant of Jesus Christ. [75] Through this man, God revealed Himself to the world.

Moses was born in the flesh, the Son of God revealed through him in power. Jesus was born in the flesh and the

Son of God declared through Him in the power of the Holy Spirit. Apostle Paul was also born in the flesh; the Son of God announced to this world through him in power by dedication.

II Corinthians tells us, "When one turns to the Lord, the veil is taken away." [76] God set us apart. Being set apart from the world does not entitle us to watch over what happens in it. This causes us to battle the temptations of sin. It is so vital for us to turn our backs to the world and place our undivided attention on God. Only then is the veil removed from our eyes. Continuing in the book of II Corinthians, "Now the Lord is the Spirit; and where the Spirit of the Lord *is*, there *is* liberty." [77] Note, the Lord is a Spirit. As we connect with Him, He gains more of us. In the process of transfiguration, the importance does not lie in us just having the Holy Spirit. Rather, through obedience and connection with God, the Holy Spirit must have us. The Holy Spirit dwells in the area where He has more of you. This is where freedom is. When you accept the Holy Spirit, you receive the fullness of the deity. The process I go through results in more of Him and less of me. There cannot be less of God. There is no such perception. God is already within you in all His fullness. All power, miracles, and authority lay inside you. The future and answers rest there. Eternity is not ahead of you, it is inside of you. Your calling is there too. You see, the answers are not in other people; they sit within.

The only way God can do more through you is when there is less of you. The less space you occupy, the more space He will fill. All of this is packaged up in your commitment to God. By turning to God, we forget our inadequacies. When Moses met God, he looked at himself and examined his abilities. From what he saw, he thought he was unable to do anything. It was at this moment God directed Moses' attention on Himself instead and promised to go with him. In order to complete his assignment, Moses had to set all his attention on God's glory.

There is no other way of transformation besides beholding God. "But we all, with unveiled face, beholding as in a mirror the glory of the Lord, are being transformed into the same image from glory to glory, just as by the Spirit of the Lord." [73] By keeping all our attention on Him, we begin to change. Jesus profoundly said He could not do anything unless He saw the Father do it. [63] Sharing the same concept, David also wrote he always saw the Lord before him. [79] Remember, that which captures your attention also holds your worship. The Bible clearly outlines, God is seeking true worshippers who will worship Him in spirit and truth. [80] The truth, in this short verse, has forever changed my life.

Apostle Paul did not speak of a prophetic time when he wrote, "But know this, that in the last days perilous times will come." [81] Instead, he prophetically informed of a time. There is a difference between the two. Prophetic times are set in place. However, you can prophetically speak of a time to come. In foreseeing a prophetic time, Paul saw the sovereign will of God. It is impossible to change a timing that is predetermined. That time has a list of reasons and consequences for it. The apostle warned of a dangerous time to come. It is not a prophetic time that is impossible to change. Instead, he prophetically explained why this time would be difficult, "Men will be lovers of themselves." [82] A trying time does not come out of anywhere due to a sudden, drastic change. There are reasons for tough times.

I believe Apostle Paul spoke of the time we currently live in. Our world today is extremely self-centered. The attention focusing on humans, not God. The words of Paul ring true as the world beckons us to focus our attention on being "lovers of ourselves". People have stopped serving in order to fulfill their own personal needs.

As you read this, you may have already experienced challenging situations. Perhaps you currently face these circumstances. This could be disease, narcotics, addictions, or any number of things. If you are struggling with a sickness in your body, then you are living in a hard time because all your attention revolves around this situation. You are in desperate need of God to reveal Himself in power. Only His power can change your current situation and the testing times you experience. Through whom, though, is this power revealed? It can only be through the person who will present himself or herself before God.

II Timothy explains self-lovers and what they do. They are, "Lovers of money, boasters, proud, blasphemers, disobedient to parents, unthankful, unholy, unloving, unforgiving, slanderers, without self-control, brutal, despisers of good, traitors, headstrong, haughty, lovers of pleasure rather than lovers of God, having a form of godliness but denying its power. And from such people turn away!" [82] Apostle Paul begins by calling such people as *lovers of self* and concludes by saying they will not be *lovers of God.* When you are a lover of God, all the attention shifts towards Him alone. It requires you to pull the attention from yourself.

Paul did not write this passage to the unbelievers. Instead, he wrote it to the category of people who had already given their life to God. The words were not intended for those who do not know God but to those who only carry an appearance of godliness. The problem lies behind all of this, is lack of power. The people, Paul speaks of, may have walked out of their own *Egypt,* however, they did not go any further. Many have walked away from the worldly lifestyle but never dedicated themselves to God. It is quite frightening to display a form of godliness yet contain all the inner qualities Paul listed. Remaining in this state withholds the power of God.

Being set apart from the world and never actually dedicating your life to God is a dangerous place to be. Some people have dedicated their life to doing ministry work for God, but they live a separate lifestyle outside of their ministry. Jesus himself said a time would come when people would kill and think they had offered a service to God. [83] This is all because they never came to know Jesus or the Father. I notice this *godly appearance,* the apostle writes about, all around. People carry a name as if they are alive, but on the inside, they are dead. I have met people who fight for holiness, yet they hardly understand that holiness is not just a form or a face. It should result in the production of fruit when we connect with God.

The issue is not in the fact that there is less of God in us, but it lies in our ego, which bulges out from within. Our 'I' is heard above all else in our heart. For God to be revealed more, we need to become less. If I still possess these polluted human qualities, it indicates I have not been transformed into the image of God. Battling for an image is a warfare for holiness. The power of God is not on the side of holiness. Instead, it is on the side of your dedication to Him.

Apostle Paul warned Timothy to stay away from people who have no power. During one of my prayers, the Holy Spirit opened this scripture to me in a new light. I read it from the bottom up, "Lovers of pleasure rather than lovers of God." [82] This text reveals we must love God in order to have power. Therefore, to behold glory and power, all attention needs to focus on seeking God.

What will occur when we look at His glory and take the attention off ourselves? What will happen when we desire His strength? What will change when we love God with all our heart? The result of this is through the process of transfiguration; all the negative characteristics will diminish and disappear. As you become a lover of God, the lover of pleasure in you will evaporate. Boasting, pride, and blasphemy will die. You will acquire new characteristics such as goodness and patience in place of slander and lack of self-control. Where you once were ungrateful, you will begin to find ways to thank others. Obedience will come first, and pride will march out the exit door. As you stop loving money and yourself, the Son of God will declare Himself in power according to the Holy Spirit.

When you pray, begin to behold the glory of God and make the choice to spend time with Him. I assure you, your negative qualities will leave your life as His qualities invade. The Spirit of God can reconstruct situations and change the time you live in. Therefore, my friend, I call you to walk further in God than the ordinary. Increase your zeal to behold His glory and His power. Fall deeper in love with God as you communicate with Him.

A life without prayer will not allow you to see anything the way it should be. When we increase time in prayer, we begin to see many poor, inner qualities that must leave our life. This course will chisel us in a way to become an answer for others around us. Operating with the power of God gives us the ability to destroy the works of the devil. These works are diseases, addictions, curses, and so on. I believe we can change the time we live in when God opens in His power. Our transfiguration will allow us to see those who are suffering. We will hear the heartbeat of God for His people and carry the same kind of compassion towards them as He does. God longs to use us to free people from a mindset of slavery and destroy all the works of the enemy. He declares Himself in power through this.

Moses was born in the flesh. He then became a slave of God so God could declare Himself in power. This also happened in the life of Jesus. He was fully dedicated and sold out to do the work of the Father. Although Apostle Paul was born in the flesh, he did not take what the flesh wanted into consideration. Instead, he beheld the glory of God. The Son of God and His power were revealed to the Gentiles through the life of Paul. Through the apostle's devotion, the works of the enemy were beat.

This is your time. I once made the decision to dedicate my time, body, and life to God. He declared Himself through His power. Transformed into His image, I grew from glory to glory in the Spirit of God. I became an answer to this generation. By working to fulfill God's plan, I actualize His vision and His desires. I bring His will to earth as it is in Heaven.

CHAPTER TWELVE

POTENTIAL

It is written, "'Eye has not seen, nor ear heard, nor have entered into the heart of man the things which God has prepared for those who love Him.' But God has revealed *them* to us through His Spirit. For the Spirit searches all things, yes, the deep things of God." [84] No one, beside the Spirit of God, knows that which is of God. Only the Holy Spirit can reveal to us what our physical eyes have not seen and our physical ears have not heard. He alone can show us things, which have yet crossed our mind regarding what God has prepared for those who love Him. These things are so much greater and wider than we can grasp. Our wildest imagination cannot comprehend even the surface. A person cannot explain these things because they go beyond the potential and ability of a human, and God prepared it for us long ago. Therefore, it refers to a work the Lord has already completed in the spiritual world. Before it ever happens in the visible world, God first completes it. He never begins anything in the physical realm until he finishes it in the spiritual.

This is another confirmation that God is both the beginning and the end simultaneously. In the book of Jeremiah it says, "For I know the thoughts that I think toward you, says the Lord, thoughts of peace and not of evil, to give you a future and a hope." [3] When we read the words *I know*, the 'I' refers to Yahweh. Our God remains Lord in every moment and throughout all eras. There is profound wisdom in this.

Because God is a Spirit, there is an immeasurable potential within Him. He is so vast we cannot fit Him into any generation or specific period. God is greater than the Heavens themselves because He created them. They are His throne of management. The earth is His footstool. He produces the physical world from the spiritual world. The magnitude of God is in the fact that He does not live in time. His creation of time itself, on the territory of earth, rests with His plan, will, and intentions. Although we function in time, God does not view the earth from a time perspective. All generations and eras exist on earth alone.

This mindset and immense perspective is a thin glass through which we can see and understand a powerful truth. This is to say, the Lamb of God was slain before the earth came to existence, having brought His entire will to completion. Beginning with the creation of the world and ending with the revelation of what is yet to come. From Genesis to Revelation, everything is already complete. Even things our physical eyes cannot see are finished. You and I are simply living out in the realm of our time in the generation God has predestined for us. Pressing forward, we draw near to the final moment. God's completion of all things, as written in Revelation, are closer than ever. His hands will accomplish His will in this timing and we will once again enter the territory of eternity. It is here God abides. The fullness, which fills everything. He is the Alpha and the Omega. He is both the beginning and the end at the same time. Eternity will never end. It is forever.

When God says only He knows the thoughts He thinks toward us, this means He sees the beginning from the endpoint. Upon seeing the end, He determines the beginning. This is the uniqueness of God's wisdom. The Bible speaks of the completed work God has prepared for us. The timing we live in links directly with His will and intentions.

When creating day one, God already existed in the juncture you live in now. He saw you. With day two and three of creation complete, God stood in both the first day created and today simultaneously. He saw it all in one moment. He knew you and the time in which you live. He saw the necessity of your generation. This illustrates the vast and bottomless depth of God's wisdom and greatness.

In the book of Isaiah, we read, "Declaring the end from the beginning, and from ancient times *things* that are not *yet* done, saying, 'My counsel shall stand, and I will do all My pleasure.'" [85] The spiritual world operates in a very different way. God has completed the end because He resides in an eternal realm. As the Alpha, He also proclaims He is the Omega. Isaiah captures this magnificent truth in the words of Scripture. God speaks on what will be completed although everything has already been done within Him. In this is His counsel and strength.

God, in the size of eternity, has placed you and me on this earthly territory to operate in what we know as time. Spiritually, everything has been completed in the eternal realm. We simply live these timed moments on earth. When God looks at you, He sees His masterpiece. A complete creation. Looking at things from this point of context, I understand the importance of my existence. I see how much God depends on me. Anything born into the visible world is a direct testimony of a completed work in the spiritual world. Your very existence proves this. Your destiny is already complete in the spiritual world. Now, you are welcomed into reality. It is time for you to live out the reason for which you were born.

Ephesians 1:4 says, "He chose us in Him before the foundation of the world." [86] In the form of a seed within God, you and I emerged into the spiritual world. We came to be in the spiritual world from within God. When God told Moses He would deliver the Israelites from Egypt, He had already foreseen the role Moses would play. Before Moses was even born into the physical world, God knew his predestination.

The story of Abraham touches an interesting detail. It mentions Abraham presented a tithed to Melchizedek, the Priest of God Most High. A contribution brought in the face of the tribe of Levi, which was still hidden within the seed of Abraham at the time. Though not yet visible in the physical world, Levi brought a certain portion to Melchizedek in the face of Abraham. The tribe of Levi already existed in the spiritual world. It is from the spiritual world that everything comes to be in the physical world.

James writes, "Of His own will He brought us forth by the word of truth." [87] Isaiah also writes, "For as the rain comes down, and the snow from heaven, and do not return there, but water the earth, and make it bring forth and bud, that it may give seed to the sower and bread to the eater. So shall My word be that goes forth from My mouth; it shall not return to Me void, but it shall accomplish what I please, and it shall prosper *in the thing* for which I sent it." [88] Everything derives from a word that carries the fullness of God in itself. As written in John, "In the beginning was the Word, and the Word was with God, and the Word was God. He was in the beginning with God. All things were made through Him, and without Him nothing was made that was made." [89] We were in God before the creation of time and He sent forth His word. If you are able to grasp this with your mindset and understanding, then prophetically I say to you, you and I are words in His Word. In His Word is a seed. When God so desired, He gave birth to us with His word. It is then He released us into this physical world through His word. We will not return fruitless but will fulfill the reason for which He released us to the earth by His word. God sent us for a purpose. Therefore, He confidently says only He knows the plans He has for us. This is because He has already determined and completed them. His desire is for you to bring fruit in your generation, for you to complete the very thing He brought you to earth.

A spoken prophetic word originates from eternity. It is capable to see your entire destiny. In Jeremiah, God speaks to the Israelites. During this time, His people were in dire circumstances. As they stood under Babylon's captivity, God spoke a word to them, telling them He knew the plans He had for them. God saw beyond their current situation. He foretold them about His intentions regarding their lives. Not only does God see the future, but He is also already there.

A prophetic word also speaks on God's objective for your life. It goes much further, deeper, and wider than the situations you face today. Sent forth to declare something about your future, it provides strength to pull you out of the things that bind you. The Word allows you to see yourself and your life through the eyes of God. It gives you a chance to see it all from His perspective. This viewpoint is nothing like what you have ever seen or heard. It is not anything that has ever crossed your mind before. The prophetic word also confirms what God has already completed.

Examining the life of King David, I believe He connected with the Holy Spirit. This is why He cherished God's presence so much. David's only request had been for the Spirit of God to remain with him. [90] The presence of God allows us to see beyond our physical capabilities. Through it, we are able to see everything in a spiritual perspective. Unlike physical eyesight, spiritual vision is transformative and correlates with our mindset. Our mentality determines what we see. Through a renewed mind, we are able to see the things prepared for us by God. Closing our eyes, we can tune in to hear what our physical ears have not heard, and see what our physical eyes have never seen. The Holy Spirit reveals this to us. A connection with the Holy Spirit opens our spiritual eyes to see what we are otherwise unable to see.

It was only in God's presence that David was able to see himself at a stage when he was still unborn. He saw himself as an embryo inside of his mother's womb. In Psalm 139, he says, "For You formed my inward parts; You covered me in my mother's womb. I will praise You, for I am fearfully *and* wonderfully made; marvelous are Your works, and *that* my soul knows very well." [91] Physically, David would never be able to see this because the soul is a sphere of the mindset. He captured this revelation with the inner world of his mind. Continuing in the passage, David writes, "My frame was not hidden from You, when I was made in secret, a*nd* skillfully wrought in the lowest parts of the earth. Your eyes saw my substance, being yet unformed. And in Your book they all were written, the days fashioned for me, when as yet there were none of them." [92] David spoke on the days already written for him in God's book. Through revelation, he captured this treasure with his inner world. He saw the completed work prior to his formation inside of his mother's womb.

I see a limitless God before me who lives in an infinite realm and speaks from eternity. "Then the word of the Lord came to me, saying, 'Before I formed you in the womb I knew you.'" [93] Notice the difference between this text and the one from the book of Psalms. David had only seen what was being formed in the womb. God, however, speaks even deeper from eternity. He came to know you before He even formed you. Knowing, on such a deep level, requires a connection. Because God knows everything about you, an assignment has been prepared for your destiny. There is work and it must be completed.

In the next part of these verses, we read the conversation between God and Jeremiah, "Before you were born I sanctified you; I ordained you a prophet to the nations." Then said I: 'Ah, Lord God! Behold, I cannot speak, for I *am* a youth.'" [94] This eye opening experience occurred in a later part of Jeremiah's life. We do not know if Jeremiah had already penciled in his own plans. Up until then, Jeremiah lived with a certain viewpoint. In a single moment God spoke, changing him forever. Jeremiah was never the same again. A word came and performed its own work in the life of Jeremiah. Presenting him with eternal hope, God spoke about his calling and predestination. God told Jeremiah, before forming him in the womb, he already knew him. Before his creation, Jeremiah had already been in God. In the spiritual world, everything was already complete. Only then did God allow him to be born into the physical world.

During the birth of Jeremiah, God already sanctified and ordained him as a prophet to the nations. The prophetic gift is often undervalued. God existed in the generation of Jeremiah before he was born into the physical world.

Foreseeing the events and occurrences that would take place, God knew there would be a need for His gift. A prophetic gift. Being inside of God, Jeremiah was chosen, ordained and sent to earth for a specific time. His purpose was to be an answer for the need in his generation. Isaiah 55 confirms Jeremiah's arrival to the world by a word released from God's mouth, "It shall not return to Me void, but it shall accomplish what I please, and it shall prosper *in the thing* for which I sent it." [95]

It is often difficult to grasp the meaning of a gift. This is because our attention is centered on one's talents and abilities. Both of these things relate to the gifting, but they are not the gift. Your gift is the true purpose of your predestination on earth. The Father sent Jesus to this earth as a gift. Through a released Word, Jesus became the flesh who dwelt amongst us. Full of grace and truth, He was a gift for the world. When the Samaritan woman encountered Jesus, He said to her, "If you knew the gift of God, and who it is who says to you, 'Give Me a drink,' you would have asked Him, and He would have given you living water." [96] In the simplest of terms, Jesus told the woman He could become the answer to her need. What He said held a deep and profound spiritual meaning. The spoken word went far beyond regular time. It entered the spiritual world. There, everything operates under a different set of laws, an eternal realm that is very real. The spiritual world is what creates the visible world.

This exact concept explains the birth of Jeremiah. God ordained him as a prophet before He formed him inside his mother's womb. God already knew Jeremiah in eternity and sent him to earth as a gift. You and I must also become an answer to our generation.

David writes, in Psalms, about bringing fruit in our due time. [97] We came from God, live in God, and will return to Him one day. Although each of us is born into our own bloodline, we all carry God's potential and designation. Our purpose is not to merely live or get by, but to be fruitful in this life. That is why God sent us out of eternity. Through Him, it all came to be.

Taken from the seed of God, He placed us into a physical body. If someone draws water from the ocean into a cup, the water inside remains ocean water. The only limitation to that water is the cup. You and I are both taken from the Spirit of God. He has no limits and is not under any boundaries of time. Placed inside a body, we now live in a physical world with the seed of God inside of us. This seed must open. It holds your God-given destiny. Throughout your life, this seed must reveal you as a gift for your generation.

Jesus spoke about the Kingdom, "The kingdom of heaven is like a mustard seed." [98] A planted seed has the ability to open, grow, and become a tree in which many can nest within its branches. A tiny seed but a garden full of potential. Picture a tiny, black apple seed in the palm of your hand. Looking at it with your physical eye, you will not be able see everything this small, raw seed contains inside of itself. The human eye is often quite limited and unable to see what God has prepared. If we do not spend time with the Holy Spirit, we cannot know the perspective God has for our life. Observing the tiny seed with question, we make a determination of ourselves based on physical abilities, *"What can I really do? I am insignificant. I am nothing but a little seed."* Unfortunately, this is typically how we see ourselves. God sees differently. He not only sees the seed, but also the instilled potential within.

Placed in the appropriate environment, the seed has the capacity to grow into an entire tree. A tree can then yield a large quantity of fruit. Within the fruit will be even more seeds. These seeds represent further tree growth. This creates a never ending cycling of trees continuing to produce fruit that contain seeds within.

Being in the wrong environment can hinder the seed inside of you. When God speaks, He does not speak to a bare seed; He speaks to the potential within the seed. God speaks beyond your circumstances. He speaks into the things that are ahead and have already been predestined for you. What God arranged, for those who love Him, may have never crossed your wildest dreams. They might be things that you have never seen with your eyes or heard with your ears.

Planted in the right environment, the seed will give life to an entire tree. When the tree yields fruit, the fruit will not go out to the people. However, people will come to the fruit to fulfill their need. The fruit on the tree becomes an answer for the need of the people and their hunger. This all comes down to you and me. We must comprehend the divine and magnificent potential, which correlates to the reason for our birth.

While on earth, we should never compare ourselves to someone else. You were born to become who God destined you to be. When He completed your destiny in the spiritual realm, He allowed you to breathe your first breath on earth. The reason He sent you is to fulfill a role and bear fruit in your season of time. He intended you to become an answer to the need of your generation. If you do not accomplish your role, of providing an answer to the questions of your time, the generation you live in may suffer. Acknowledging the importance of your calling is essential. We must come to see ourselves through the eyes of God.

The Holy Spirit once spoke to me saying, "You determine what will occur around you and after you." He continued to show me many young people who suffered because they were unable to find themselves due to one reason; the previous generation did not accomplish its goal. I have come to understand our problems are not in narcotic drugs, sexual sin, drunkenness, depression, frustration, or rejection. It is in the absence of predestination. The greatest problem is that people have missed the main goal. I want you to understand that God wants you to complete your destiny more than you may even want to.

If you were to take an apple seed and place it on a table to grow, the results would be ineffective. Returning a year later, you will notice that the seed never sprouted because it was in the wrong environment. Suppose you left the seed in the same place for another decade. Coming back, you will find the seed dried up. Many people have never been able to reveal themselves only because they never made it to the right environment. The opening of potential directly ties to the soil. This is why many see themselves as a dry seed from a physical viewpoint.

Myles Munroe, a man of God, once said, "The wealthiest place on the planet is just down the road. It is the cemetery." [A1] Millions of people lay dead, never having become who they ought to have been. Left as a seed, they did not open their full potential. The graveyards are full of music never composed. Bestselling books never written. Pastors who never started a church. Hands, which never picked up a paintbrush to create a masterpiece. Sadly, the richest place on earth is the cemetery. It is a ground full of graves.

In the book of Matthew, we observe a moment where Jesus taught the multitude, "When He had called the multitude to *Himself*, He said to them, 'hear and understand:

Not what goes into the mouth defiles a man; but what comes out of the mouth, this defiles a man.' Then His disciples came and said to Him, 'Do You know that the Pharisees were offended when they heard this saying?' But He answered and said, 'Every plant which My heavenly Father has not planted will be uprooted. Let them alone. They are blind leaders of the blind. And if the blind leads the blind, both will fall into a ditch." [99] Jesus was not speaking about physical eyesight. He was referring to spiritual vision. He stated any plant not planted, by the Heavenly Father, would be uprooted. This includes your thoughts and mentality. Further on in the passage, Jesus says, "Are you also still without understanding?" [100] Here, He references the mindset. In Luke, Jesus warns His disciples about the leaven of the Pharisees. [101] He did this because the formulation of our mindset is also through teaching. In those times, the Pharisees were teachers. The book of Romans says, "Do you not know to whom you present yourselves slaves to obey, you are that one's slaves whom you obey, whether of sin *leading* to death, or of obedience *leading* to righteousness? But God be thanked that *though* you were slaves of sin, yet you obeyed from the heart that form of doctrine to which you were delivered." [102] We all carry the responsibility to decide which teaching we give ourselves to. The teachings we hear are a determining factor of our inner belief and understanding. They define our point of view. Seeing how God sees gives our seed the ability to open up in its fullness.

Jesus is the Word and plants the Word as a seed. He explains the parable of the seed in the book of Matthew, "When anyone hears the word of the kingdom, and does not understand *it,* then the wicked *one* comes and snatches away what was sown in his heart. This is he who received seed by the wayside." [103] Our mindset forms once our ear hears the

Word. As explained in the parable, Jesus plants the Word as a seed within the soil; the soil is our mind. When Jesus preached about the heart, it represented the soil as well. The heart of a person is the spirit that was in God before the creation of the earth.

A person's thoughts move in the spiritual sphere, which occupies the mind. Our mindset is given to process thoughts inside our brain. The Spoken Word is able to sculpt our thinking. This is crucial as we see everything through our inner world. Therefore, it is our inner vision, which determines the degree we will open up and become the person God destined us to be.

CHAPTER THIRTEEN

VISION

A person may not become who God envisioned them to be for a number of reasons. One reason, which holds people back from discovering God's divine perspective for their life, is their mentality. Teachings greatly influence our way of thinking. Surrendering yourself to God's way of teaching is imperative. This is because it will correctly form your outlook and determine your inner worldview. Ultimately, your mindset will set you up to become who God destined you to be on earth.

There are various human opinions surrounding you and majority of them are inaccurate. The only opinion, about you, that is valid and true comes from the One who created you. When we connect to the Holy Spirit, He reveals the depths of God to us because He permeates through everything. The Holy Spirit created you. He predestined your life and sent you to this earth. God ordained you and He knows everything about you. This is why no one else knows the things of God except for the Holy Spirit. Apostle Paul writes, "For what man knows the things of a man except the spirit of the man which is in him? Even so, no one knows the things of God except the Spirit of God. Now we have received, not the spirit of the world, but the Spirit who is from God, that we might know the things that have been freely given to us by God." [27]

There are three types of spirits: the human spirit, the spirit of the world, and the Spirit of God. The spiritual always dominates the physical. It always comes first. You and I are spiritual beings. We do not have a spirit; we are a spirit.

The human spirit carries a humanly form of teaching. This teaching establishes priorities and values on what the human eye can see in the physical world. When we disconnect from the Spirit of God, our mindset forms on logic. This logic fully depends on the visible world.

Scripture defines the spirit of the world as "lust of the flesh, the lust of the eyes, and the pride of life." [104] This spirit also carries its own form of teaching, which affects the human mind. Circumstances and situations in the visible world are the teacher. This includes everything you see, feel, touch, and experience. Those that surround and communicate with you play their role as well. You learn as you live your life. As a result, the spirit of the world influences the mindset of humans.

The Spirit of God carries His own form of teaching, which completely differs from the other two. It is the only true way of teaching. You see, truth is a Spirit and God is the Spirit of Truth. When we come to understand this Spirit, He sets us free. God liberates us from a mentality of slavery, which is the belief of limitation. Jesus say, "You shall know the truth, and the truth shall make you free." [105]

With edification, the Spirit of God teaches us so that we ultimately become who God determined us to be. In Corinthians, Apostle Paul writes, "Now we have received, not the spirit of the world, but the Spirit who is from God, that we might know the things that have been freely given to us by God. These things we also speak, not in words, which man's wisdom teaches, but which the Holy Spirit teaches, comparing spiritual things with spiritual. But the natural man does not receive the things of the Spirit of God, for they are foolishness to him; nor can he know them, because they are spiritually discerned. But he who is spiritual judges all things, yet he himself is rightly judged by no one. For "who has known the mind of the Lord that he may instruct Him?" But we have the mind of Christ." [106]

What God gifted to us is true and complete. It explains who we really are, not someone's opinion of us. Understanding the truth about our identity and discovering God's plan for our life delivers us from jealousy, pride, arrogance, and rejection. The truth sets us free. It rescues us from all lies, human opinions, and the evil thoughts of the devil.

By coming into the true light, which is God alone, I am able to see light. It is here I can live my life in correlation to this light. When we allow the Holy Spirit to teach us, He influences our mind so we are able to renew our thinking and come to know the will of God. Jesus came to earth as the true Light. [107] He is the one who edifies every person born into the world. The world we live in influences our beliefs. It also forms our vision and the worldview we carry within. The Bible tells us Jesus must instruct us with the true light. Through His light, we are able to see ourselves clearly.

Jesus was a word, which came from Heaven. In Him was life and this life was the light of men. In Greek, the word used in this passage is *logos*, meaning an expression of an idea. It is a released thought. "In the beginning was the Word, and the Word was with God, and the Word was God." [107] The Word are thoughts of God, His ethos, and His desires. This is what became flesh and lives amongst us. The

Word began to teach us in order to form our way of thinking. Jesus Himself came to educate us by revealing the mindset of the Heavenly Father.

I have many thoughts. In order for me to speak these thoughts, I must release a word. Releasing the word influences the mentality of those listening to me. This is why Jesus became the Word. By doing so, He brought God's mindset to life in order to influence our mentality. In His light alone, we are able to see a true light that enlightens every person entering earth.

Jesus connected with the Holy Spirit. In the book of John, He says, "The words that I speak to you are spirit, and they are life." [108] Through the words of Jesus, the Holy Spirit teaches those who listen. The Holy Spirit also reveals the plan of God. In Matthew, it says, "From that time Jesus began to preach and to say, 'Repent, for the kingdom of heaven is at hand.'" [109] The word *repent* means to renew your mind.

Jesus proclaimed the message of God's Kingdom, which is within the Holy Spirit. To be able to see ourselves in God's Kingdom, the Holy Spirit must teach us how to think in this method. An untransformed mind is incapable of grasping the vision of God. The logical way of human nature will always consider this concept as foolish.

What God has for you is greater, wider, and bigger than you can comprehend. It is impossible to explain in average, human terms. To see the will of God, we must see through spiritual eyes. Only those with a renewed mind, who think as Christ, will be able to understand and accept what God has for them. By teaching the Kingdom message, Jesus uprooted everything not planted by the Father in the minds of people. This message has a purpose and encompasses the entire earth.

God created the heavens and the earth. Religion is unable to see the entire earth throughout all generations as God can. Therefore, people cannot find themselves and their calling, or open their potential, in a religious system. Jesus warned people, instructing them to beware of the teachings of the Pharisees because they affect the mentality. Your time and destiny is only be found in the Kingdom of God. Returning to the mentality of the Kingdom, you will be able to see yourself through God's vision.

In Matthew writes, "It has been given to you to know the mysteries of the kingdom of heaven, but to them it has not been given. For whoever has, to him more will be given, and he will have abundance; but whoever does not have, even what he has will be taken away from him." Continuing in verse 19, Jesus says, "When anyone hears the word of the kingdom, and does not understand it, then the wicked one comes and snatches away what was sown in his heart. This is he who received seed by the wayside." [110]

Although the seed is planted, inside of the heart, it must affect the mind. Jesus affirms, when the word of the Kingdom is spoken, a person must lean in to understand. In other words, they must renew their mind; otherwise, they will not be able to bear fruit. The devil is well aware of this. As soon as the Kingdom message is spoken, it influences the mentality of the person listening. The message of the Kingdom is exactly what Jesus preached. By renewing your mind, to understand, you edify, within, to open up. Knowing this, the devil comes to steal it immediately. When a person hears and does not attempt to understand, the enemy instantly snatches it away and anything shrugged off, he steals.

How does this influence our mentality? Every spoken word directly affects the thoughts. The thoughts you have carry their own images. Because each word carries a particular image, it forms your worldview. For instance, let us take the word *apple*. When you hear this word, you can close your eyes and see the form of an apple. The only variance is every person will envision a different kind of apple. Some visualize it to be red while others picture it green. Everyone sees it completely different in shape or size. Now imagine the word with more detail. Instead of just *apple,* you hear *a big green apple.* What happens then? Simultaneously, everyone will see the same image in his or her mind. When we see the same object, we can speak about the same idea. Apostle Paul says, "God is faithful, by whom you were called into the fellowship of His Son, Jesus Christ our Lord. Now I plead with you, brethren, by the name of our Lord Jesus Christ, that you all speak the same thing and that there be no divisions among you, but that you be perfectly joined together in the same mind and in the same judgment." [111]

From the start, everything began with relationship and communication. The book of Ephesians tells us He is the One God and Father of all. He is above all and in all of us. [112] Because we are connected in one Spirit, He teaches us the same concepts. Learning the same message allows us to see in unison, which is why Jesus imparted the Kingdom Message. He preached it so everyone's inner world or mindset can transform. When each of us understands in a similar way, we find ourselves in the concept of God's Kingdom, which encompasses His entire will.

When Jesus taught the Lord's Prayer, He said, "Your kingdom come. Your will be done on earth as it is in heaven." [113] The Kingdom of God is in heaven. His will encompasses the entire earth and the heavens. When Jesus descended from heaven, He taught about the true light, which are God's intentions and ideas. Having heard this message, He teaches us to see through God's point of view.

The devil understands the way this works and does everything in his power to hold this information back from us. He tries different approaches to keep us from returning to the teaching of the Kingdom of God. The enemy hates it when the Holy Spirit edifies our mind to understand. He knows communication with the Holy Spirit is what enlightens and teaches people the right way. The devil fears this. Jesus is the purest theology. He is the divine teaching. The enemy constantly fights to keep people from hearing about the Kingdom of God. When we do not know, we hold ourselves back from fully opening up and becoming fruitful. However, the very event that the devil despises is what glorifies the Father. True worship is not in words but in your predestination.

Imagine holding the latest smartphone in your hand. If the functions are not used, it does not bring glory or honor to the creator of the phone. Commendation is awarded to the creator of the device when all the functions are used to their capacity. Other people watch, in wonder, as the functions are utilized for their created purpose. The phone is an answer to a need. The more it is used, the more it uplifts and brings recognition to the mastermind behind it. Applying this concept to scripture, we see that bearing fruit glorifies the Father.

This is my desire, and God placed a vision inside of me regarding this book, that through it, each reader would thirst to seek divine things. That a hunger would rise to develop a personal relationship with the Holy Spirit, who edifies the mind. I pray it broadens our inner worldview to a level of godliness. You are a seed ready to be planted into the right soil. By sprouting in the soil, you will become who He created you to be. God called you to be fruitful on earth, to be an answer for the need of the millions surrounding you by accomplishing the goal He specifically has for you. One day, you will stand before Jesus and receive a reward for your obedience and completion of what he predestined for you.

CHAPTER FOURTEEN

RENEWAL

Every one of you reading this book is at a different stage in your life. You might be fifteen years old; or you may be twenty, thirty, forty, or fifty years young. Each of us has our own life experience. Some of you may have received an education for a specific profession. While others might currently be running a business. You may be not be working but, instead, are committed to ministry full-time. Regardless of your circumstance, this book is in your hands. Perhaps you have been feeling uneasy as you continue to live day by day. You walk in dimness with no light ahead of you. The loud whisper constantly echoes in your mind, reminding you that you are not fulfilling your role. There is a lack of certainty. Many unanswered questions lay piled up inside.

As you read each page, the insight sparks a desire to live the rest of your life in accordance with God's will. Although the priorities and values of this world still press at you, inside there is an intense burst of energy stirring up to fulfill God's plan. If you examine your heart, you will see God is directing you to the true path and setting you free from an unfruitful life. I have faith the rest of this book will push you out of the spot you are currently stuck in. It will practically guide you toward God's direction for your life.

The previous chapters carry colossal meaning. They are like pieces to a big puzzle that fill in each gap and greatly influence our way of thinking and point of view. They formulate our inner worldview, known as the System of Faith. This system intertwines with our way of thinking. My prayer is that all of these chapters become your teacher and influence your thinking.

The System of Faith determines the way you live on earth. If you believe correctly, you will live correctly. Forming yourself through divine teaching is crucial because it directly influences your faith system. You will eventually see the fruit of this displayed in the way you live. If we live our life purposefully, it will testify our time was not wasted.

"Do you not know that to whom you present yourselves slaves to obey, you are that one's slaves whom you obey, whether of sin leading to death, or of obedience leading to righteousness? But God be thanked that though you were slaves of sin, yet you obeyed from the heart that form of doctrine to which you were delivered." [102] One question stands out while reading this passage. To what form of teaching have you enslaved yourself? Whatever the answer may be is the one whom you obey. When you submit to obey, your inner desires come forth to action. Obedience directly corresponds to your inner system of faith. This derives from the form of teaching you submit yourself to.

Many forms of teaching is accomplished by using words. It takes faith to believe these words, as faith comes from hearing. Your mind becomes influenced by what you hear. As a result, your faith is demonstrated through action. We all carry a responsibility for the life we are given and the form of teaching we choose to subject ourselves to. Whoever forms our mindset, through teaching, is the one whom we will obey.

The verse we read above indicates all of us were once slaves of sin. To *sin* means to miss the target or focal point. The system of this world is a system of slavery. It forces a person to live a certain way and miss the main objective. The Bible tells us the lust of the eyes, the lust of the flesh, and the pride of life, are not from the Father. Instead, they contradict the will of God. All these things are parts of the sinful nature influencing the subconscious. This nature withholds a person from the truth and keeps them from liberation. The system of the world is sinful nature and it has its own form of teaching.

If people do not seek the Kingdom of God, or form a relationship with the Holy Spirit, they still survive somehow. However, they are unable to see how the worldly influences form their thinking through temporary values. The priorities of this earth pull out what they need from within those individuals. Obeying this system, sin enslaves them. As a slave to this lifestyle, they miss the target of what God predestined for them.

Radical change begins inside of you. The first part to come out of a mother's womb, into the visible world, is the head of a baby. Relating this concept to our lives, we realize all radical change begins from the form of teaching we obey. It all starts from the head. A transformed mindset, or a different way of thinking, brings change. Because of this, Jesus preached about the Kingdom of God. The teaching of the Kingdom changed the way people thought. Hearing the message, they accepted a new way of life, which Adam initially lost in the Garden of Eden.

When Adam was in the Garden, the heavens were connected with the earth. Due to disobedience, Adam disconnected himself from the influence that heaven had on earthly territory. Lucifer came to earth illegally. Through deceit, he took away the authority belonging to humankind. Upon creating man, God gave him dominion. [9] He gave man the power of rulership. Because of one man's disobedience, Lucifer entered the sphere of the skies with power. This sphere is between heaven and earth. The devil took away the dominion, which is the power to rule over the earth.

The system of earth has the power to control. Invading the mindset of a human, it takes action through the physical body. Before Jesus came to earth and won the victory, people were under the power of a sinful system. While living under the slavery of sin, people continually missed their life's purpose and did not complete God's will. The power is in the Kingdom of God as it is able to influence our sub-consciousness. It can form our thinking.

Let us observe what the scripture says about what Jesus accomplished. In the book of Colossians, it says, "Giving thanks to the Father who has qualified us to be partakers of the inheritance of the saints in the light. He has delivered us from the power of darkness and conveyed us into the kingdom of the Son of His love, in whom we have redemption through His blood, the forgiveness of sins. He is the image of the invisible God, the firstborn over all creation. For by Him all things were created that are in heaven and that are on earth, visible and invisible, whether thrones or dominions or principalities or powers. All things were created through Him and for Him. And He is before all things, and in Him all things consist. And He is the head of the body, the church, who is the beginning, the firstborn from the dead, that in all things He may have the preeminence. For it pleased the Father that in Him all the fullness should dwell, and by Him to reconcile all things to

Himself, by Him, whether things on earth or things in heaven, having made peace through the blood of His cross." [114]

Through the cross, God made peace and reconciled the earthly with the heavenly. We now have life on the other side of the cross. Some may wonder what exactly happened on the cross. Jesus, the Son of God, took away the power from all authorities and systems of government, bringing them to shame because He triumphed over all. Jesus took the power away from Lucifer, which was once lost in Eden by Adam. By dying on the cross, Jesus became the door through which we can enter into the Kingdom of God once again. When we step through the door, we can live life on the other side of the cross. This means we can live in the Kingdom of God. Because of His victory, the system of this world no longer holds any power.

The grace of God abides on the other side of the cross. Here, we receive everything we do not deserve, given to us by grace as a beautiful gift from God. A completely new world exists on this side of the cross. The Holy Spirit and a renewed mindset await us here. Everything Jesus finalized on the cross is now a foundation for us as believers. It is a fundamental point from where new life streams out.

Today, the Holy Spirit acts on behalf of the Father. Continuously, He completes the work on the other side of the cross. The mindset of the Kingdom is in the Holy Spirit. He takes action from the point of Jesus' victory. Through the cross, God set us free from the power of darkness and brought us into the Kingdom of His Beloved Son. Now we must learn how to live on the other side of the cross.

In Matthew it says, "But seek first the kingdom of God and His righteousness, and all these things shall be added to you." [115] A transformed mindset lies on the other side of the cross. The power of resurrection is there. When Jesus resurrected from the dead, He raised us with Him too. [116] He placed us within Himself in the Heavenly realm. Having the mindset of Christ, Jesus put us in a position where we now have the power of the Kingdom.

Jesus took all authority and power back. The book of Matthew tells us, "Jesus came and spoke to them, saying, 'All authority has been given to Me in heaven and on earth.'" [117] Everything Adam once lost have now been given back to us so we can fulfill the will of God. We must bring down what is in heaven to earth.

In order for us to comprehend how God's power works, we must first understand how His Kingdom operates. The preaching of Jesus always begins with repentance. Repentance is what signifies a transformation of the mind. To accept the true way of life, which is on the other side of the cross, we need to seek the conviction of God's Kingdom. In Jesus Christ, you and I already have it all.

As already revealed, transformation of your mind will occur when you kneel down to seek the Kingdom of God. Jesus said the Kingdom of God is like a mustard seed, which is able to grow and become a big tree. [98] The mechanism of how the Kingdom message affects us breaks down into a process. This spiritual process is what the Holy Spirit grows within us. The Kingdom of God is compared to leaven for this reason. While asking the Holy Spirit to teach us, as we seek this Kingdom and study it, the message of it modifies, or leavens, our thinking in a unique way.

This message is like a seed, which takes root within and captures our entire inner world. We become consumed by a different way of thinking. The seed grows inside and we begin to see through God's point of view. God's vision lays within the Kingdom teaching. Bending down to understand the Kingdom message stirs new desires within us. These desires then develop into actions. Ultimately, we come to obey the teachings to which we give ourselves.

Dear friend, I want you to know there is an entirely different lifestyle waiting you on the other side of the cross. Jesus became a door to it through the cross. We can now live in the inheritance of God and in the mindset of His Kingdom. We have the ability to operate through the power and authority of God's Kingdom. His will is the same on earth as it is in Heaven. It holds your designation and role on earth.

I urge you to study the teachings of Jesus, found in the four Gospels of the New Testament. You will find his only focus was on the Kingdom of God. Not only do I encourage you to read those passages, but also to spend time alone with the Holy Spirit. He has the outlook of the Kingdom and can renew your mind. Because the Kingdom works as leaven, it will expand within you until it changes your entire mindset. Then, having a different viewpoint will develop a different system of faith within you. This will bring forth change and new feelings. It will give you confidence, courage, and new ideas. You will begin to act according to the mindset the Holy Spirit stirs inside of you.

CHAPTER FIFTEEN

INFLUENCE

John the Baptist preached in the wilderness of Judah saying, "Repent, for the kingdom of heaven is at hand!" [118] Often, people accentuate the passages where Jesus said John did not perform any signs but still considered one of the greatest prophets. [119] When we study the prophets of the Bible, our focus tends to be on what the prophets accomplished in their time instead of what they were distinguished and purposed for by God. Examining the Word, we read, "The law and the prophets were until John. Since that time the kingdom of God has been preached, and everyone is pressing into it." [120] Although we pay attention to the miracles and actions of the prophets, true greatness is not found in those things. The significance of a prophet has always been in their predestination.

Throughout the Old Testament, prophets testified about the coming of Jesus Christ, the King, to earth. Yet it was John the Baptist, the last prophet of the Old Testament, who was the one to foresee and prepare the way for the coming of the King. If we study the concept of a Kingdom, we notice a reoccurring theme; prior to the arrival of the king, a messenger will always come first. This messenger is a voice proclaiming the coming of the king. John the Baptist was this voice. His distinction had been in his calling, found in his destiny and prepared by God.

Every person, walking this earth, will one day stand before the King of kings and receive their heavenly reward. Obedience and the fulfillment of our predestination will determine our reward. Jesus says, "Everyone to whom much was given, of him much will be required," [121]

Your God-purposed destiny may differ from the one He intended for those around you. Suppose He appointed you to influence and bring one million people to Christ in the visible realm, whereas He called me to bring one hundred people. The magnitude of the reward given to us would be within the obedience to our calling and not the size of it.

Unlike the visible world, the Kingdom of God operates completely different. In the physical world, we may serve in a greater measure; however, God gave each of us our own amount of strength, which we cannot compare to each other. There are certain people who we must influence.

The destiny for you might be to bring a million people to Jesus Christ, yet you only manage to bring one hundred thousand. In the visible world, your achievement will appear far greater than my achievement and seem more successful, according to human understanding. However, God only called me to bring one hundred people. The reward in the eternal realm is based only on our obedience and fulfillment of our destiny.

If I lead ninety people to Christ in comparison to your one hundred thousand, my reward will be bigger because I came closer to completing my calling. Although people will be astonished with the greatness of your ministry, since it appears larger, God measures everything based on our obedience to fulfill His calling. He pays attention to how close you and I come to accomplishing our destiny. Since I fulfilled almost one-hundred percent of my calling, my reward would be larger.

The greatness of John the Baptist was not within any miracles but in the fulfillment of his calling and predestination. When compared to all other prophets, he was the closest to the King. Others testified about the coming of Jesus however, John the Baptist was the one who prepared the way. He completed his role. The prophets before John could only dream of seeing what he was able to see. Before the coming of Jesus, John preached in the wilderness of Judea saying, "Repent, for the kingdom of heaven is at hand!" [118] Even when Jesus had already come to earth, he continued to preach this message.

Regardless of your calling, it must carry a message. John the Baptist was a gift to this world. Being a prophet, John's gifting was his platform to preach about the Gospel of the Kingdom. Jesus also came to earth as a gift and served the needs of the people around him. Through healing and deliverance, He brought peace. Jesus was an answer and used this pulpit to preach God's message. It does not matter what God has called you to do, He made a place for you on earth and provided the territory from which you can influence others. Your calling is a gift for this world to use as a platform from which you preach the message about the Kingdom of God.

A young girl once approached her pastor saying, "Pastor, I want to fulfill God's will on this earth for me." "No problem," the pastor responded. "Jesus said to, 'Heal the sick, cleanse the lepers, raise the dead, cast out demons. Freely you have received, freely give.'" [122] Shrugging her shoulders, she said, "But I feel God is calling me to be a doctor." The pastor replied to her without missing a beat. "Go ahead! Become a doctor and preach about the Kingdom of God. Heal the sick, raise the dead, and cast out demons." Sometime later, another young man approached the same pastor and expressed the desire to fulfill God's will for his life. Excited, the pastor's response was the same. "That is so great! Now go ahead and preach about the Kingdom of God! Heal the sick, raise the dead, and cast out demons." Although he understood the words of his pastor, the young man went on to explain that he actually felt a calling to be a lawyer. Once again, the pastor smiled and answered, "That's no problem at all. Become a lawyer for that is what God is calling you to be." This is your gifting and your territory of influence from which you must carry out a message. Preach the message of the Kingdom from that platform and heal the sick, raise the dead, and cast out demons.

When John the Baptist preached this message, it stirred a reaction in the people surrounding him. People approached John asking, "What shall we do then?" [123] As you read this book, you may find yourself in the same boat. You may not understand what you should do next. As I preach the Kingdom message around the world, I am constantly asked one question, "What should I do next?" What is it then we should do from the place we stand today? John the Baptist responded to the people in the following way, **"He answered and said to them, 'He who has two tunics, let him give to him who has none; and he who has food, let him do likewise.' Then tax collectors also came to be baptized, and said to him, 'Teacher, what shall we do?' And he said to them, 'Collect no more than what is appointed for you.' Likewise, the soldiers asked him, saying, 'And what shall we do?' So, he said to them, 'Do not intimidate anyone or accuse falsely, and be content with your wages.' [112]**

Your gifting provides you the opportunity to give to others. In order to serve and carry out the message, you need strength. The words of John offer insight into where we can begin and what our next steps should be. When people holding different positions, titles, and territories of influence approached John the Baptist, he did not tell them to dump everything and leave it behind. Instead, by preaching the Kingdom message, he taught them about a transformed mindset. He demonstrated how the will of God links with the entire earth and its system of governance. John the Baptist wanted to show people they have a sphere of influence in their designated territory. Through it, they must be the salt of the earth and bring light to it.

Jesus said that, "You are the light of the world." [32] Our duty then, is to carry the light to this world. There are varieties of worlds surrounding us, such as political, sport, business, medicine, and religious worlds. As believers, we must carry the light of God into all of these spheres. When those around see our good deeds, they will glorify our Heavenly Father. Using a transformed method of thinking, John the Baptist instructed everyone to see his or her specific scope as a territory of influence. The territory of influence does not exist to fulfill selfish interests, but to influence the world through good works. Each person's position allows him or her to serve others through the opportunities they are given as well as preach about the Kingdom of God. By doing so, the light of God spreads throughout.

A process currently unfolds in your life through which the Holy Spirit guides you and takes you straight towards your destiny. Until that time comes, apply what you have heard regarding the Kingdom message and the importance of your calling. Go out and use your territory of influence to serve people and preach the Gospel of the Kingdom to everyone around you.

When Jesus approached John the Baptist, He insisted on being baptized by John. [125] Back then, John was the one who preached about the Kingdom of God. The Greek translation of the word *baptism* means to be immersed. Jesus did not go to the Pharisees or the Sadducees to be baptized because they preached their own form of teaching. During the time of Jesus, Caiaphas was the Priest. However, Jesus did not want to be baptized by him either. He did not associate Himself with his form of teaching. Instead, Jesus wanted the Father to uproot everything He did not plant. Unfortunately, the Pharisees had already sown a great deal into the people. Their teachings were like leaven, overtaking the mindset of those who listened to them. Knowing this, Jesus warned His disciples against the teachings of the Pharisees and went around preaching the same message John the Baptist taught. The passage in Luke confirms the Kingdom message began to spread after John the Baptist came into the world. [120]

My friend, the Kingdom of God holds immense power. It is capable of changing your thinking and helping you see your territory as the influential platform, to disperse the Good News. To influence the entire earth, God needs the calling of every single person. A religion cannot fit the calling of everyone within itself, only the Kingdom of God can do this. You and I need to become the salt of the earth and the light to it. As you continue to read this book, allow the Holy Spirit to lead you forward into your destiny. Make a choice to serve people exactly where you are at by preaching the Kingdom message to them. Remember, your territory is your personal stage from where you hold power to influence the destiny of many.

CHAPTER SIXTEEN

PROCESS

Every one of us undergoes our own process. Jesus led me through my process and He will take you through yours. Jesus, leading by the greatest example, says, "I am the way, the truth, and the life." [126] True life is found in our God-given destiny and only truth is able to free anything holding us back from your destiny. Jesus is the way and leads us through the path.

Teaching His team of disciples, Jesus ushered them to enter their destiny. The process, to destiny, is unique for every individual. Although each disciple had a different mindset, shaped by their specific upbringing, Jesus pulled them into their God's calling. This team eventually created the church.

In the book of Mark, we read a fascinating encounter between the disciples and Jesus. The disciples found themselves in an interesting situation, which held significance. "Then He came to Capernaum. And when He was in the house, He asked them, 'What was it you disputed among yourselves on the road?' But they kept silent, for on the road they had disputed among themselves who would be the greatest." [128]

The conversation Jesus addressed had taken place between the disciples as they walked. The road in this passage represents a lifelong process. As He walked ahead, the disciples followed in step behind Him. Because Jesus is the way, He guided His disciples along the path. On this path, they discussed among themselves to determine who of them was greater. The meaning behind this is applicable to what goes on in our world to this day. In the lifelong process we walk through, we continuously try to determine who is better. This desire exists inside every person. Somewhere deep within, each one of us wants to feel greater. In the visible world, we try to express our level of greatness by buying nice houses, driving luxurious cars, or leading in ministry.

Jesus did not stop his disciples in the process of their discussion, instead allowed them to speak so they could hear themselves. Nowhere along the way did He stop them or rebuke them for their words. This serves as a significant teaching objective regarding fatherhood and leadership. By staying silent, as they walked, Jesus gave the disciples space to be open.

The house Jesus and the disciples walked into symbolizes the presence of God. When they had entered the house, He finally addressed their conversation making it clear He heard their words but allowed them to discuss everything anyway. In a position of leadership, it is essential to bring a person into a state of understanding and not cause them to close-off. Instead of crushing their inner aspirations, we must create an atmosphere in which they come to a different understanding and see things from God's perfect perspective. As a leader, Jesus brought the disciples into God's presence, the house, and then questioned their discussion.

Throughout my life, I have noticed we try to prove a point by putting someone down or raising ourselves up through bragging. When we come into the presence of God, with a pure heart, we radically experience Him. Here, God gives us His intuition and allows us to see through His eyes. Looking at things His way often brings us embarrassment for the way we behave. Jesus did not force anything on the disciples. Instead, He brought them to a place where they saw their foolish attempt to prove which of them was worthier in the eyes of people. In the presence of God, they realized what they had done and were ashamed.

The teaching method Jesus used was to sit the disciples down and instruct them. The Word says, "He sat down, called the twelve, and said to them, 'If anyone desires to be first, he shall be last of all and servant of all.'" [128] This passage does not say He rebuked them or told them their earlier discussion was wrong or unnecessary. It does not say he questioned why they even strived for greatness. Instead, Jesus simply explained what one should do to become first. He paved a higher path before them, showing them a process God takes people through in order to raise them up. Jesus confirmed the importance of being first and holding a position of greatness.

Jesus explained whoever desires to be first, must be last of all. Being first holds great responsibility but does not mean we are better than anyone else. The position makes us responsible for what will occur after us. Jesus is greater than all. He is the head of the body, and because He is first, He is the firm foundation we stand on. Within a family, a husband is also the first or the head. In the beginning, God created Adam as the first man. [129] Then, He brought Eve to Adam as his helper. Adam being first does not mean he is better. Instead, it places a weight of responsibility on him because he decides what will occur after him. It is a great privilege to be first, and God desires you to stand in position; however, you will be the one to determine what happens after you.

Being first has always been God's promise. In Deuteronomy, God gave commandments to the people and expressed He wanted His people to be first, the head, and not the tail. [130] This position is momentous, only mature people can hold it. In Ecclesiastes it is written, "Woe to you, O land, when your king is a child," [131] We can apply this to today's government and say, *"Woe to you, O nation, when an immature leader, or someone who is unable to serve people, holds the presidential position."* In the same sense, working under an immature boss is extremely difficult because they use their position to serve their own needs. These kinds of people do not understand their position is given to them as a platform to serve. Taking this to our schools today, it is unsettling when a teacher, who is head of the class, uses his or her influence in a negative way. Instead of encouraging the students, they misuse their position and discourage them.

Hearing the conversation of the disciples, Jesus understood God instilled their longing for greatness. In our life, we often forget God uses a path to bring us to such a position. Jesus says whoever desires to be first must become last among everyone. God showed me this exact process at the very beginning of my journey.

Because being last holds so much importance, we need to understand what it looks like practically. Imagine you come to church for a weekly service. After the sermon, the pastor dismisses all the members but turns to you and asks you to stay after service. Hearing his words, you understand you will be the last person to leave. Everyone goes home, and you are left alone. The pastors request for you to clean the building. Your initial reaction may be to say, "Why me?

Why not someone else?" However, Jesus not only said the first should be last but also servant of all. When you become a servant, you no longer have any reason to create excuses and cannot ask these types of questions. A servant does not grumble or seek someone to blame but rather completes the tasks asked of them.

Choosing to stay back to fulfill pastor's request is a process of work that is invisible. No one is going to pat you on the back or tell you what a great job you did. Neither will you hear anyone saying how amazing it is to have you as a part of the church. The work, truly done for God, begins when you serve with no one around to watch. Being a servant takes away the need to hear the praise of people. The hidden key behind this victory is in the process through which God Himself raises you. Eventually, the things you do in the unseen will become seen and known to everyone around you. We must continue to do the unseen work as if we are doing it for God alone, and not wait for praise or recognition.

Jesus brought up two key phrases in the Gospel of Luke, to be faithful in the little and faithful to someone else's belongings. [132] The first part of His words indicate the size of what we do does not matter. Whether it seems grand or small in the eyes of people is not important. What matters most is you doing everything before God and not people. Those in this world need us to serve.

The second phrase in this passage is about remaining faithful to someone else's belongings or vision. The local church you attend is the territory of your pastor's calling. God positioned him there to lead the people of your congregation, and you are a part of your pastor's ministry. Before leading you to your territory of influence, God will mold you in another place. Therefore, be faithful where you are, "And as you wish that others would do to you, do so to them." [133] The instruction does not change depending on whether you find yourself in a church or a place of business. Treat others the way you want to be treated in your position of influence. God placed those people as the first in their specific area, and you must be faithful while you remain under their authority. Make the decision to become a servant and last of all.

Being faithful to that which is another's means I must be fully obedient to the instructions given to me by the head of that ministry or business. I remember a moment from my life regarding this principle. When I repented, I began to serve in a local church. I refused to remain in one area and sought new opportunities to help in various ways. I was not able to wrap my mind around how I could possibly love God and yet not love the church He placed me into. How could I not when the Scriptures tell us the church is the very body of Jesus Christ?

In Galatians we read, "The heir, as long as he is a child, does not differ at all from a slave, though he is master of all," [134] From the moment you are born, you became a son or daughter of God and an heir. Although defined as heirs, there is a process you and I must go through to mature and reach the destiny set before us.

I believe the path to our destiny is through the local church. God places people into the body of Christ, and it is where they grow and mature. In the next verse of Galatians, it says you are "under guardians and stewards until the time appointed by the father." [136] A specific time has been appointed by God to prepare you and then place you into the position of your predestination. Because you will be first in your area, God wants you to be mature and equipped to serve people without drawing attention to your interests. He desires for those around you to testify on your behalf, the influence and example you have been on their path toward destiny.

When I met Jesus, He told me where He would lead me but never specified when it would take place. Similarly, an angel appeared before Zechariah and informed him he would have a son, but Zechariah did not believe the words he heard. Because of his disbelief, the angel responded saying, "You will be mute and not able to speak until the day these things take place, because you did not believe my words which will be fulfilled in their own time." [1] Your Heavenly Father chose a time at which He will place you into your position of destiny. From this place, salvation will be brought to others, and through it, the Son of God will be glorified.

In my own life, I wanted to accomplish everything the pastor of my church asked of me. I had a desire to be faithful with everything placed into my hands, and to me, every small task mattered. Without waiting for someone to tell me what to do, I found areas in which I could serve. It was my intent to become a servant, and I did not waste time questioning the tasks needing to be complete. I did not wonder why others did not want to do the work but simply did what I could and asked God to show me where else I could be of use.

This process pulled me into my appointed timing, and because I remained faithful in the little, choosing to be last, I reached my destiny point. Having gone from position to position while serving, I was stretched in my abilities. Eventually, it all led me to the territory of my calling from which I am now a blessing to the nations.

CHAPTER SEVENTEEN

LESSONS

Joseph had a personal relationship with the Father. One night, God showed him a vision through a vivid dream, "Now Joseph had a dream, and he told it to his brothers; and they hated him even more. So, he said to them, 'Please hear this dream which I have dreamed: There we were, binding sheaves in the field. Then behold, my sheaf arose and also stood upright; and indeed, your sheaves stood all around and bowed down to my sheaf.' And his brothers said to him, 'Shall you indeed reign over us? Or shall you indeed have dominion over us?' So, they hated him even more for his dreams and for his words. Then he dreamed still another dream and told it to his brothers, and said, 'Look, I have dreamed another dream. And this time, the sun, the moon, and the eleven stars bowed down to me.' So, he told it to his father and his brothers; and his father rebuked him and said to him, 'What is this dream that you have dreamed? Shall your mother and I and your brothers indeed come to bow down to the earth before you?'" [136]

In this vision, Joseph saw the direction God was guiding him. Each part of the dream was symbolic, and he saw the position prepared for him was one in which he would be first; Joseph was destined by God to be the head. Seeing this, the difficult step for Joseph was to believe the dream and accept it for what it was. Just like any of us who hear the voice of God, he needed to humble himself and receive it.

Today, the greatest humility will often appear to be pride in the eyes of those around. Humbling yourself by committing to fulfill God's desires is the greatest form of humility, and it is His will we do this. When Joseph shared his dream with his brothers, they questioned whether he would really rule over them. The most humble way Joseph could have answered them was by saying, *yes* and confirming it would happen. However, imagine how inaccurately people would view this response.

Joseph had to undergo his life process between the age of seventeen and thirty to get to his destiny. Only after going through the process, did he reach the appointed position provided by the Heavenly Father. The Bible says, "Until the time that his word came to pass, the word of the Lord tested him." [130] The Word of God pulled Joseph into his position. Moving him forward, God placed Joseph into the status of being first.

Further, in the story of Joseph, we read, once he became the head of the nation, men came to obtain wise counsel from him. There is no evidence that Joseph completed any schooling nor did he obtain a degree, so his wisdom had to come from God alone. The greatest wisdom then is acquired by maturing in God.

Maturity correlates with the process through which God takes a person. The life Joseph lived to reach his destiny and calling is full of lessons we can apply to ourselves. From a physical standpoint, Joseph appeared to be last. After throwing him into a pit, Joseph's brothers sold him as a slave. Arriving in Egypt, he was bought by Potiphar and taken to his new master's house. The combination of all of these events brought him into the position of last place, and Joseph could have become angry at the entire world for the way he was treated. Humanly speaking, he had every excuse to be angry and remain furious, accomplishing nothing in his life.

Reading this story, God directed my attention to several verses I believe summarize the major lessons of Joseph's life. "The Lord was with Joseph, and he was a successful man; and he was in the house of his master the Egyptian. And his master saw that the Lord was with him and that the Lord made all he did to prosper in his hand." [138] Clearly, Joseph had a personal relationship with the Father. The verses indicate the Lord was with Joseph. The passage also hints that Joseph was faithful in his work during this part of his life process. He did not sit or observe what was going on. Instead, Joseph accomplished everything needing to be done around him. In the position of being last, he became a servant of all and fulfilled the needs he saw. Joseph's motive was to do the work for God alone. His brothers had left him behind, and his father was not there to thank him for his efforts. Because Joseph did the work as for God, the Lord gave him success. You cannot become successful if you do not do anything; begin doing something as Joseph did. Start working in an area where there is a need.

God showed me Joseph was placed over someone else's business in the house of Potiphar, "So Joseph found favor in his sight, and served him. Then he made him overseer of his house, and all that he had he put under his authority. So it was, from the time that he had made him overseer of his house and all that he had, that the Lord blessed the Egyptian's house for Joseph's sake; and the blessing of the Lord was on all that he had in the house and in the field. Thus he left all that he had in Joseph's hand, and he did not know what he had except for the bread which he ate." [139] The house Joseph lived in was not his own and yet, he remained faithful in this stranger's home and did everything needing to be done. His faithfulness is what eventually placed him in the position to oversee the entire house of Potiphar. Finding favor in the eyes of a man, Joseph became successful and God blessed him.

God opened a revelation for me; many people remain in the house of Potiphar because they have grown to be good at what they do in this place. However, the greatest enemy for your destiny is yesterday's success. Many people do not let God take them further because they have grown comfortable in their current space. Do not allow the house of Potiphar to keep you back from your own appointed time by the Heavenly Father. Being loyal to things, which belong to others, is a part of God's will for your life. However, it is dangerous to get stuck there. The success you establish should not hold you back from moving into God's destiny for your life.

In the life of Joseph, God created situations carrying Joseph out of the house and forward towards his destiny. His unlikely circumstance led him straight to prison. Although Joseph may have looked at this as a moment of crisis, God saw it as an opportunity to bring Joseph into his predetermined position. "Then Joseph's master took him and put him into the prison, a place where the king's prisoners were confined. And he was there in the prison. But the Lord was with Joseph and showed him mercy, and He gave him favor in the sight of the keeper of the prison. And the keeper of the prison committed to Joseph's hand all the prisoners who were in the prison; whatever they did there, it was his doing. The keeper of the prison did not look into anything that was under Joseph's authority, because the

Lord was with him; and whatever he did, the Lord made it prosper." [140]

Despite Joseph being locked away, God still gave success in another sphere of management. By the looks of it, it seemed everything to be spiraling downhill. He was stuck in the lowest of all places; confined in prison. No matter what things seemed like on the physical level, this was his path to elevation. Joseph was destined by God to be first so the land of Egypt could thrive. The people surrounding him needed to be blessed by his position and maturity.

Joseph had several opportunities from humans to be lifted up. However, elevation does not come from the east or the west. God brings one person down and raises another. For this reason, let it be He who leads and moves you forward through divine path. If you ask, the Holy Spirit will form you from the inside. This way, you will not seek the weak, human methods for promotions or make any compromises to benefit.

Regardless of Joseph's condition or lack of comfort, he continued to serve through any opportunity he was given. The Bible clearly underlines his heart for serving in the later part, "It came to pass after these things that the butler and the baker of the king of Egypt offended their lord, the king of Egypt. And Pharaoh was angry with his two officers, the chief butler and the chief baker. So he put them in custody in the house of the captain of the guard, in the prison, the place where Joseph was confined. And the captain of the guard charged Joseph with them, and he served them; so they were in custody for a while. Then the butler and the baker of the king of Egypt, who were confined in the prison, had a dream, both of them, each man's dream in one night and each man's dream with its own interpretation. And Joseph came in to them in the morning and looked at them, and saw that they were sad. So he asked Pharaoh's officers who were with him in the custody of his lord's house, saying, 'Why do you look so sad today?' And they said to him, 'We each have had a dream, and there is no interpreter of it.' So Joseph said to them, 'Do not interpretations belong to God? Tell them to me, please.'" [141]

Joseph was fully aware the butler and the baker had once been by the King. In this moment, human opportunities for advancement were right beside him. Both of the dreams carried entirely different meanings. One of them was good, while the other had a terrible ending. Even so, Joseph did not make any compromises. In instances before and the one at hand, he let God elevate him. The interpretation of the dreams had to be accurate, and Joseph did not receive any personal benefit from translating them. The dream with a good ending happened, and the butler found himself before the king once again. Although the interpretation of the baker's dream meant he would be killed, Joseph stood firm and explained the sad truth to the man. He did not settle for anything lower than the truth and waited for God to raise him instead of trying to do so himself through this situation.

The Heavenly Father has an appointed time, which He set for you. Using His divine methods and ways, He takes you through a process leading to your destiny. God's desire is for you to submit yourself to His form of teaching and allow the Holy Spirit to rule your life. Because you are under His Lordship, He alone should be the one to promote and elevate. The Lord should raise you up and not the hands of a human.

While you develop a personal relationship with God, remain faithful in the little and in that which belongs to someone else. Do not seek justice but become a servant of all and when you reach a place in which God gives you success, continue to move forward. The halfway point should not stop you from moving toward your God-given destiny. My prayer is for you not to remain in the house of Potiphar, but be ready for God to take you further into His appointed timing. Just like in the life of Joseph, there will come a moment in which you too will step into the position of being first. By being faithful and managing the things he was given, Joseph reached his point of destiny. The vivid dream God had shown him as a young boy finally came to pass, and through his position, he became a blessing for many nations.

CHAPTER EIGHTEEN

FULLNESS

Looking back, I remember the nights of prayer meetings at my house. God moved in such a mighty way among us, and the number of people attending multiplied. Before long, we ran out of space in our small home and moved the meetings to the church building where I am still a member.

It was during this time the ministry, God had called me to, began to grow and gain success. The Holy Spirit spoke to me and gave me a strategy, which I needed to implement in the city. He instructed me to hold a revival service for the entire city on the last Sunday of every month. By this time, many of those around began to see God was with me and His blessing was on me. The success was evident because God was behind it all. Seeing this, people stepped up to serve alongside. From there, it did not take very long for a team to form around me.

Receiving His word for city services, we began working with all our abilities. Everyone performed their part and we creatively expanded into all areas and spheres to make these services a reality. Quickly gaining momentum, the ministry grew, becoming very influential. Every month the building brimmed with hearts hungry for God's movement. The services influenced young people while countless others repented and received deliverance as our team continued to serve. Because of these services, those who attended formed small groups, meeting weekly in each other's homes.

Time passed, and I began to notice the youth looking up to me, listening to my words over the words of our senior pastor. I understood something needed to change otherwise the youth ministry would soon cause great division and split the church. If this continued, a new church would be formed apart from this one.

Needing direction, I locked myself away to pray. As I listened, God spoke to me. He said, "I have not called you to divide the church. I called you to be a blessing for My body and the local churches." During my prayer, God opened His desire to lead me further, and everything finally came together to make sense. If I focused on the current situation, I would be closing my eyes to God's predestination. His plans for me were greater than this. While learning to obey His voice, my call was to be a blessing for the body of Jesus Christ. God also said He wanted to release me through the body in order to fulfill what He assigned for me.

Approaching the leaders around me, I announced that from that day forward we would all obey the Senior Pastor and execute everything He wanted us to carry out. I emphasized that because we were a part of this church, we were to abide by its order. There was absolutely no desire in me for anyone to listen to my words over the Senior Pastor. Success was undeniable but the moment had come for me to sacrifice my *Isaac*. Although in the visible world this ministry had accelerated and considered to be flourishing by many, I understood sacrificing my current success was essential to reach my God-given destiny.

As the 2010 year began, I strangely felt as though the power and energy, I once had for youth ministry, suddenly vanished. No longer did it feel like my own and at that moment, it was more far-reaching and foreign than ever. The condition within me was odd and difficult to understand. Only a day ago I possessed the strength and vision for the ministry with ideas and energy I could not contain. Then, in what felt like a second, something abruptly changed within and a feeling of emptiness settled in. What once had been so precious to me was now as distant as a stranger was.

In that time, it seemed most inconvenient and improper, but God began to speak to me through the words of Scripture. Tuning my ears to what He was saying, I knew the moment to launch a worldwide ministry had come. But where to begin? I had nothing to build from and was all by myself. With no resources or people, I saw no human way to start. How could a worldwide ministry possibly begin from an empty slate? The questions increased. By praying and spending time with God, I understood my appointed time had come. Before this moment, God never spoke on the exact timing of my destiny, but once it was near, it felt so right. The time had come and the time was now.

My wife and I only had one request before God. This request was for us not to begin our ministry at the wrong time. We wanted to wait on the Lord and have Him go ahead of us. Seeing the hand of God on our lives was of utmost importance for Natasha and me. In addition to this, our desire was for the church to give us their blessing when the time did come. It had never been my intention to shut the door in anyone's face or prove I am right when I began my ministry. The last thing I wanted was for people to consider me as some *great guy* God was calling forth. I continued doing the work God set before me and trusted there was a perfect time for everything.

Knowing God's timing had come, a personal struggle in my Garden of Gethsemane began once again. Standing between the visible and invisible, I understood I had to take a step of faith and enter a place I had never been before. When Abraham obeyed the call on his life, God brought him out. He went into the unseen, and I knew I must do the same. As I increased my time in prayer, God continued to speak to me through dreams. In one dream, I saw God place His hand on me. Not only did I see this, but I also felt it physically. Anointing began to run through my body the instant God placed His hand on my head, and I heard a voice saying, "Go, I am with you. Do what I have called you for." Waking the next morning, a confidence I could not explain filled me and gave me confirmation the time had indeed come. God was calling me to move forward.

The visible circumstances in my world repeatedly told me I was not strong enough and I was incapable of entering my destiny. They shouted that I was alone. A constant stream of questions filled my mind, causing me to wonder how it would all work out. *Who would invite me to serve? How would each event play out?* Fighting for victory, the battle between my inner self and the visible world waged on.

During this time, a group of missionaries came to my house for a prayer gathering. Beginning to pray, the Spirit of God came on us so powerfully. The missionaries began prophesying to me. The prophetic word had been very strict. I understood God, my Father, spoke directly to me as His son and called me forth to complete His will. God informed me He would, one day, ask me of everything He had entrusted to me and I must obey His voice, and go forward to complete what He called me for. When the time God has appointed for you comes in your life, you will clearly recognize it. I assure you the Word of God will find you. He will speak to you regarding this from within and corroborate His words using external sources. This is precisely how it happened in my life.

The concluding part of this transitional chapter in my life was the moment God spoke to my wife. It was the final confirmation that my timing had come. During the entire process, leading me towards my calling, I did not just ask God to keep my wife by my side. I wanted more than this. I pleaded she would become one with me concerning the vision on our lives. One night, God showed her a prophetic dream. Usually, I am the one who God speaks to through prophetic dreams, and Natasha rarely receives them at all. Rather than rush to share what she had seen, she waited several days before addressing the dream. That year, the last verification I needed to move forward came from my wife and the vision she saw.

In her dream, Natasha found herself standing in line before the throne of God. The row of people was very long and one by one, she watched as they approached the throne to give an account. An angel would come up, take the next person in line, and bring them before the throne. Standing right behind me, Natasha witnessed an angel take me by the hand and walk me up to the throne. As I stood there, she observed the expressions playing on my face. Although she could not hear what the angel said, she watched as my face sank down in disappointment. The angel's conversation with me was a lot longer than those who had gone before, and it appeared as though something was being explained to me. Seeing this from afar, Natasha trembled and began asking God to open her ears so she could hear the words spoken to her husband. Answering her prayer, God allowed her to listen to what was being said to me. The last phrase the angel declared to me there was, "You will go to Heaven, but you did not complete that which you were destined for."

She awoke from the dream, frightened. At this time, Natasha had no idea what was going on inside of me. She only knew God was calling us higher. Having opened my heart to her before, she knew something would happen in our lives and the prophets God sent to our house were a sure sign. It was my inner battles, which I did not speak to her about. As the days passed, my wife finally sat me down to talk. While I listened to the details of her dream, everything inside of me shook. I came to a startling realization; the scariest part in life is not to die, but never to fulfill God's destiny.

Unable to eat or sleep for days following our conversation, the details of the dream repeatedly spiraled through my mind. Kneeling before the Father, I prayed, "God, I am all yours. Do all you want with me. I do not know how it will come to be, and I do not know what awaits me. I do not even know where to begin. Please, tell me." My Father heard my voice, and in response to my plea, God provided me with a few directions.

First, He said, "I will go before you and construct your schedule." His instructions were clear. I was not to try to sell myself to others or push towards progress using my own strength. Rather than advertise myself, I needed to allow Him to lead. God was to be the boss of my daily schedule. He would be the one to open doors and send me to cities and countries He saw fit. Moreover, the measure of my obedience would determine the measure of my anointing. That anointing would then bring forth success in my ministry.

The second direction, from God, was for me to make sure all the necessary documentation for the ministry was prepared. Taking heed, I developed a partnership system and prepared all the required paperwork for a non-profit organization. Everything concerning administrative work was squared away and ready to go.

The third and final instruction was to gather the pastoral team at my church. Having agreed to all the directions set before me, I worked to accomplish the final one. I came to church, one day, and gathering the team of pastors, I explained what had occurred.

As they listened, I shared my revelation with them of how God is the light and there is no darkness in Him. Because of this, we must also learn to walk in the light. In addition, I explained that our conversations with others should always be clear, open, and transparent. There should be nothing to hide. When I had finished sharing my heart, my pastor and the team agreed to bless me for the ministry God called me.

Having completed everything He told me to accomplish, I waited for the rest of God's directions. Unaware of what to do next, God showed me an unusual image as I slept. In the dream, I found myself in Germany. The following morning, I clearly understood God was calling me to go to Germany. Interestingly enough, the only person I knew who lived in Germany was my older brother. This did not deter me and I did not hesitate because I had no doubt God called to go there. However, the only problem was the timing; it was right before Christmas. It seemed like a peculiar time because I knew everyone was busy with the holiday season at hand. Even though it was inconvenient, I brought the news to my wife and discussed it with her. Listening to my explanation, she said that if God showed me this dream, then I must go.

Without further delay, I called my brother. After our conversation, I purchased a plane ticket and flew to Germany. Arriving to this unfamiliar country, I met with the pastor of the church where my brother was a member. Having spent some time in discussion, the pastor invited me to speak at the church service the following Sunday.

That Sunday, service lasted much longer than usual. It began at three in the afternoon and went on for six hours. As I prayed for those in attendance, the Holy Spirit began to move, healing and delivering people. A particular testimony, from the evening, captured my attention as a man grabbed the microphone to share what had happened to him.

The man resided in Germany and he was saving money to fly to the city of Almaty. Once he arrived, he planned to hire a hitman to kill someone who wronged him in some way. For so many years, the devil lied to this man and deceived him with this bitterness. With just one week remaining before he had scheduled to go to Almaty and commit a horrendous crime, God brought him to this service. Up until that day, his life purpose anchored in revenge and retaliation. That Sunday, the Holy Spirit touched him, fully delivering him from all the anguish he endured. Standing before the congregation and clutching the microphone, he testified he no longer wanted to fly anywhere. Instead, he desired to use the finances to serve God's Kingdom.

Listening to the words of this transformed man, I saw the reason behind my oddly timed trip in his tear-filled eyes. The purpose for my flight to Germany, right before Christmas, stood before me in the form of a saved soul! At that moment, I could not help but wonder what would have happen if I disobeyed the voice of God or postponed it for a later time.

The word spread quickly, and people invited me to their homes so I could serve and pray for healing and deliverance. When I returned to the states, a minister contacted me and asked me to meet with him. He explained God had told him to record an episode for his television show with me during which I would share my personal testimony. I agreed to this. Once recorded, the video was sent to different locations.

Invitations began to come from all sorts of sources. I was amazed. Doors opened, flooding me with opportunities and God completely reformed my schedule. Everything started to happen so quickly, and I firmly acknowledged the fact I would have been incapable of fulfilling the need if I had not obeyed God. The importance of completing all of the administrative work in advance was something only God could have foreseen. Requests for me to serve in other cities continued to arrive. As I traveled, more signs and wonders took place. As each service ended, lives changed before my very eyes.

In the midst of it all, God spoke to me saying I must invest into starting my own television broadcast. He wanted my attention to focus on the media ministry. Because of these recorded episodes, new doors swung open and introduced me to far more than I ever thought possible.

In the beginning, I was afraid to speak on the topic of finances and found it embarrassing. I did not know how the ministry would be financed, but I trusted God would take care of it, since this was His ministry and not mine. The partnership opportunity for our organization was prepared however, I still held back on speaking of it.

After a service at one of the local churches, a young man approached me and asked how he could support the ministry on a monthly basis. This question came from someone I least expected, and when he named off a large sum of money, I nervously directed him to a representative of the partnership ministry. He and his wife immediately completed the form and began to provide monthly support. Another incident caught me by surprise in a similar way when a check arrived from a woman, Irina, who lived in Colorado. Along with her material contribution, she had sent a letter explaining how God had urged her to become a monthly financial partner. I had never met or even heard of this person and yet, she had reached out to take part in our ministry.

Using these generous donations and many others from all around, God showed me I must not be afraid to speak about this partnership. I was to do my part in speaking, and God would work in the hearts of the people. Like a spider web, people from all over joined us and became a part of this vision. The donated finances support the distribution of God's Word through my ministry and continue to do so today. People frequently approached me to inform they are called to become a part of what was going on and it all seemed too good to be true. Feeling as though I was watching everything from the sidelines, I was fully aware God was working in the midst. I knew He was making it come together for the sake of His name. He directs us on the path of righteousness.

What began in 2010 has only increased in power and force throughout the years. Today, the team of Flame of Fire Ministry and I fly to many countries. Together, we lead crusades, schools, and conferences; impacting the nations. Not only do we travel abroad, we also serve through television broadcasts at our central studio location. This powerful media tool is used to reach many of those we may never have the opportunity to see face-to-face. I can continue to list the incredible events taking place however, I believe they are just the beginning of the vision God revealed me when I was with Jesus.

I remember the historic moment I experienced when I returned to a very familiar place: the old, wooden steps. The starting ground of my journey in pursuit of a divine relationship. It was not long ago when I drove back to the apartment complex where I once lived. Sitting in my car, I caught sight of the spot where I had sat a countless number of times. It was there, on those steps, I spent so many of my evenings.

Looking out at them that day, a significant experience began to occur. That which took place is almost too difficult and complex to put into words. I was momentarily given the opportunity to see my young, 22-year-old self, seated on the bottom of the staircase.

Two Andrey's met each other's gaze. Andrey from the past, who unknowingly sat looking into the distance, wondering how his life would turn out and the current Andrey; who runs a worldwide ministry. Somehow, the old Andrey looked me in the eyes, and I instantly felt all the worry and unanswered questions that weighed him down. His thoughts sprang up as he wondered, *"How will life evolve? What does the future hold for me? What is the meaning of life? Who am I?"* Each one of them, a little siren permeating the still air.

As I stood in the present, blooming in my calling, I peacefully looked back at the young Andrey in distress and out of my mouth came a simple response. Andrey spoke to Andrey; from the present into the past, and I said, "Do not be afraid, just continue. You can do this."

NOTES

All scripture text taken from the New Kings James Version (NKJV) Bible, unless otherwise specified in citations.

1. Luke 1:20
2. John 11:38
3. Jeremiah 29:11
4. Exodus 3:14
5. Matthew 4.4
6. Luke 4:4
7. Ephesians 3:20
8. James 2:17
9. Genesis 1:26
10. Psalm 115:16
11. I Peter 4:10
12. Genesis 2:18
13. Isaiah 6:8
14. II Corinthians 3:17
15. Ephesians 4:16
16. Acts 17:26-28
17. Joshua 1:8
18. Psalm 46:10
19. Romans 12:1-2
20. I Corinthians 6:19-20
21. Genesis 32-22-32
22. Jeremiah 29:11
23. John 10:110
24. Jeremiah 1:5
25. Psalm 139.13
26. Psalm 139:16
27. I Corinthians 2:11-12
28. Luke 21:34
29. Romans 8:13

30. Psalm 18:34
31. John 10:10
32. Matthew 5:14-16
33. Matthew 9:38
34. Matthew 4:18-22
35. John 4:34
36. Romans 8:28-29
37. Galatians 4:19
38. Ephesians 4:13
39. John 3:30
40. I Corinthians 6:17
41. Colossians 1:9
42. Colossians 1:10
43. II Peter 1:3
44. Matthew 6:6
45. Psalm 23.3
46. Luke 4:18
47. Exodus 2
48. Exodus 3:1
49. Acts 7:22
50. Revelations 22:11
51. Exodus 3:2-5
52. Leviticus 6:12
53. Romans 12:11
54. Exodus 3:6-12
55. Exodus 3:13-14
56. Deuteronomy 18:15
57. Colossians 2:15
58. Joshua 1:1-2
59. Romans 1:1-2
60. Romans 1:3-5
61. John 14:9
62. John 12:49
63. John 5:19-20

64. Matthew 26:53
65. Philippians 2:8
66. John 18:4-5
67. John 17:26
68. Matthew 9:35
69. Luke 8:54-55
70. Luke 9:16
71. John 18:6
72. John 18:5
73. Galatians 1:15-16
74. Romans 15:18-19
75. Romans 1:1
76. II Corinthians 3:16
77. II Corinthians 3:17
78. II Corinthians 3:18
79. Psalm 16:8
80. John 4:23
81. II Timothy 3:1
82. II Timothy 3:2-5
83. John 16:2
84. I Corinthians 2:9-10
85. Isaiah 46:10
86. Ephesians 1:4
87. James 1:18
88. Isaiah 55:10-11
89. John 1:1-3
90. Psalm 51:11
91. Psalm 139:13-14
92. Psalm 139:15-16
93. Jeremiah 1:4-5
94. Jeremiah 1:5-6
95. Isaiah 55:11
96. John 4:10
97. Psalm 1:3

98. Matthew 13:31
99. Matthew 15:10-14
100. Matthew 15:15
101. Luke 12:1
102. Romans 6:16-17
103. Matthew 13:19
104. I John 2:16
105. John 8:32
106. I Corinthians 2:12-16
107. John 1:1
108. John 6:63
109. Matthew 4:17
110. Matthew 13:11-12, 19
111. I Corinthians 1:9-10
112. Ephesians 4:6
113. Matthew 6:10
114. Colossians 1:12-20
115. Matthew 6:33
116. Colossians 2:12
117. Matthew 28:18
118. Matthew 3:1-2
119. John 10:41, Matthew 11:11
120. Luke 16:16
121. Luke 12:48 ESV
122. Matthew 8:10
123. Luke 3:30
124. Luke 3:11-14
125. Matthew 3:13-15
126. John 14:6
127. Mark 9:33-34
128. Mark 9:35
129. Genesis 2:7
130. Deuteronomy 28:13
131. Ecclesiastes 10:6

132. Luke 16:10-12
133. Luke 6:31
134. Galatians 4:1
135. Galatians 4:2
136. Genesis 37:5-10
137. Psalm 105:19
138. Genesis 39:2-3
139. Genesis 39:4-6
140. Genesis 39:20-23
141. Genesis 40:1

A1. Munroe, Myles. "The wealthiest place on earth is the cemetery." November 10,2014. Retrieved from https://www.thecable.ng/wealthiest-place-earth-cemetery--memorable-munroe-quotes

Made in the USA
Columbia, SC
22 December 2018